LAW OF ATTRACTION

UNLEASH THE LAW OF ATTRACTION TO GET
WHAT YOU WANT FROM THE UNIVERSE

JONATHAN GREEN

Edited by
ALICE FOGLIATA

DRAGON GOD BOOKS

Copyright © 2018 by Dragon God, Inc.

All rights reserved.

Simultaneously published in United States of America, the UK, India, Germany, France, Italy, Canada, Japan, Spain, and Brazil.

All rights reserved. No part of this book may be reproduced in any form or by any other electronic or mechanical means – except in the case of brief quotations embedded in articles or reviews –without written permission from its author.

Law of Attraction has provided the most accurate information possible. Many of the techniques used in this book are from personal experiences. The author shall not be held liable for any damages resulting from use of this book.

Paperback ISBN: 978-1718088276

Hardback ISBN: 978-1947667112

TABLE OF CONTENTS

Don't Go it Alone	v
1. What is the Law of Attraction?	1
2. How is Your Thinking Affecting Your Life?	3
3. Yes, You Can Control Your Thinking!	8
4. Mindfulness	17
5. The Vital Significance of Gratitude and Positive Thinking	21
6. Choose to be Happy!	34
7. Thinking About the Universe	43
8. Strengthening the Mind	52
9. Meditation	68
10. The Principles of Visualization and Materialization	84
11. Right Action	93
Let's Soar Together	101
More Information	103
Found a Typo?	105
About the Author	107
Books by Jonathan Green	111
One Last Thing	113

DON'T GO IT ALONE

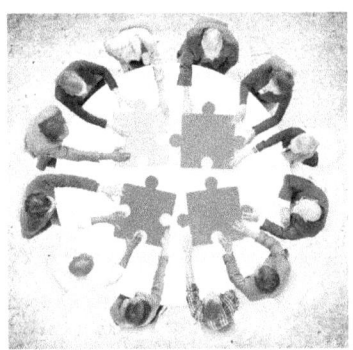

The hardest part of personal growth is going it alone. When you are in isolation, the night can seem too dark, and success can seem so far away.

We often quit right before we could experience our biggest success. Join something bigger than yourself where you can get the support, feedback, and guidance you need to achieve your desired success.

Please join my FREE, private Facebook group, filled with supportive people on the same path as you!

https://servenomaster.com/community

This is a great place to chat with me daily, share your experiences with the exercises and find a supportive group of people who are all on the same journey as you.

1
WHAT IS THE LAW OF ATTRACTION?

If you bought this book, chances are that you have heard of the law of attraction before. You almost have to have your head buried in the sand or be living under a rock for the last ten years not to have heard about this principle. Millions of people have bought books and watched movies about the law of attraction.

It is a popular philosophy, but it is most popular when you are only taught half of the system. The law of attraction is composed of two critical components and one underlying concept. The underlying concept is that the things we do affect the universe; our thoughts, actions, beliefs, and mindset radiate out into the universe and cause a reaction. From this core belief, we have the two steps of the law of attraction.

Most people only learned the first half of the law of attraction. The first step is that if you focus on something hard enough – if your belief, your desire, and your focus are strong enough – the universe will give that to you. That sounds wonderful, doesn't it? If the law of attraction were this simple, every single person in the world would have a

Ferrari sitting in their front yard. That is the beautiful, fun part of the law of attraction, but it is not enough. It is only half of the equation – the glamorous half.

The second half of the law of attraction is that you must combine the right action with the right belief in order to bend the universe to your will. As we go through this journey together, you will see how the power of changing your beliefs can and will affect the universe around you very quickly.

As you work through the drills and exercises in this book, you will see actual results from your experiments over the next few weeks. This is not a process that requires six months of hoping and wishing for something to magically appear in the mail. This is not the magical version of the law of attraction where you wish for more money, your uncle dies, and you finally get an inheritance check in the mail. This is not designed to be one of those cautionary tales that warn you to be careful what you wish for. Instead, we are designing a system and a process that will get you the things you want and bring your personality and your mindset into alignment.

2

HOW IS YOUR THINKING AFFECTING YOUR LIFE?

A re you in control of the things you think about? Are you the master of your mental dominion or do your thoughts and emotions often sway you, and you feel like you are just along for the ride? Do you sometimes feel like you are on a ship without a captain?

One of the most empowering elements of the law of attraction is that you can take control of your thought life and your destiny. You can again become the captain of your ship, and you can use that position to get the things you have always dreamed of.

In our culture, we often hear people blaming their bad behavior on everyone else; we hear it so much that we begin to believe it ourselves. "It is not my fault; the Twinkies made me do it. It is not my fault I grew up affluent and have disdain for other people; it's my parents' fault for raising me too wealthy. It is not my fault; I was depressed, and I did what I had to do."

We are so used to people using these defenses in ridiculous court cases that they begin to enter the zeitgeist of our culture. We start to believe them, and juries start to agree,

"It is not your fault you killed twelve people; you grew up rich and have disdain for poor people."

We justify bad behavior because, as a culture, we love to give away responsibility and blame our emotions or other third parties for our lives. The problem is that if you blame the rest of the universe – if you blame other people and emotions for the things that go wrong in your life – you have given away all your power to correct the course. If you read any of my other books, you are very familiar with the idea that you can be in control of your thoughts and emotions. We are going to dig deeper into that and look at how this specifically applies to using the law of attraction to get the things that you both want and deserve.

Test: How Much Control Do You Currently Have Over Your Thinking?

1. Do you tend to see thoughts as things that just come into your mind and you have no control over?

a) Yes, I think so.

b) No.

2. Do you ever find yourself distressed or tormented by thoughts and seemingly unable to get rid of the thoughts that are causing you so much sadness?

a) Yes, I do.

b) No.

3. Are you able to exert control over your thinking in order to have a different emotional response to situations in your life?

a) No, I'm not.

b) Yes, I am.

Results: the more "a" answers you chose, the lower your level of control over your thinking. If you chose one or more "a" answer, don't worry! By the end of this book, you will have the knowledge and tools you need to control your thinking more than you have probably ever imagined.

Below are some reflection questions. Like all exercises in this book, please complete these questions in what will be your Law of Attraction Journal. This Journal can be an actual notebook or a computer file. Choose at least three of these questions to answer. The Law of Attraction Journal is something very special; it is a notebook you are going to keep with you and use alongside working through this process. I know there's a very good chance that you bought the digital version of this book or the audiobook. In that case, grab a little notebook and write down your questions, answers, and experiences as you work through this process. When we learn, the more senses we use, the better we remember things.

The most powerful way to remember things is to write them down. In Japan, to read the newspaper you have to know three thousand different characters, called Kanji. Children learn these characters in school by writing them down over and over again; it is a painful method, but it works. Our method is not going to be that radical, but the more you write down your answers to these exercises, the better.

Part of it is that we are going to go back to our early exercises later on in this process, so you can see how far you have come by going back and assessing where you are today. If you just think the answers in your head or even say them out loud, when you come back in six months, you will not remember a single answer. If you write them down, your answers are set in stone, and you can accurately gauge your progress and get more positive affirmation for yourself.

Writing down your answers increases the odds of your success significantly.

Reflection Questions

For your first activity, answer three of these questions in your Law of Attraction Journal.

1. Think back on your life; have there been experiences in your past where your thoughts made things worse? Did you realize it at the time or is it a revelation now and you only notice it using hindsight? For example, you get called to the principal's office, and you keep imagining all the terrible things that can happen and how much trouble you are going to be in. When you get called in to talk to the principal, you find out that you are not in trouble at all. You imagined a problem far worse than it was, and your mind got ahead of itself.

The emotion you are feeling at the time, especially a strong, negative emotion, can dramatically color how we respond to situations. Jealousy, anger, hatred, exhaustion, angst, and anxiety make us react poorly and make situations worse. When the person you are starting to date does not respond to your text message for a few hours, if you are feeling nervous or anxious, it is very possible that you will react too quickly and kill things. We all know that sometimes you have to wait because maybe the person is just in a meeting or busy with something.

2. Have you ever been told that while you cannot always control the world around you and the things that happen to you, you can control how you react to them? How did it make you feel when someone told you that at the time? Did it make you feel like bad things are happening and you're powerless? Or did it make you feel empowered? This is

something we are going to build on as you work through this course.

3. Are there some specific things you are going through right now, such as challenges or complications that you are trying to overcome and deal with? Is having a little better control of your thought life going to help you get through them? Are there experiences you could improve if you could just take control of your thoughts?

4. We looked at the past, and we looked at the present; now look at the future. Are there future scenarios things you might have to deal with where you can specifically see how having a little firmer control of your thought life will help you to deal with them better, improve your reactions and come out with a better result on the other side?

3

YES, YOU CAN CONTROL YOUR THINKING!

You can become the master of your thought life. The very first aspect of our process is working on a belief. Beliefs affect our thoughts, and our thoughts affect our behavior, so rather than trying to alter our behavior, we are going to act on the root cause and focus on beliefs.

The very first belief is that you are in control of your thoughts and you are in control of your emotions. I am going to share with you seven different techniques you can use to strengthen your mind. Just as we train, exercise, and sweat to strengthen our bodies, discipline, effort, and repetition can strengthen our minds. We can develop mental skills just as we develop physical skills, and your thought life can become stronger and more powerful.

1. Become an observer of your own thoughts

The simple process of putting a step in between you and your thoughts will give you a great deal of control. For example, you are mad about something. In the moment, you are so mad you start yelling at someone special in your life and tell them how angry they have made you. But if we just take a moment to observe ourselves, we realize, "I am really mad, and my anger is driving me to say these things." This gives us an extra second or two to think about what we are about to do before we do it.

Before we can ask you to change what you do in these moments, we first have to become aware of what is driving your thoughts. We act differently when we are happy, mad, or sad; we interpret information and act towards people differently. Our assumptions and preconceptions affect how we interpret and absorb information.

If a doctor tells me I am overweight and I don't have motivation keep me alive longer, it stings a little bit, but I take it and try to improve my behavior. If someone we are attracted to tells us that we're fat, it hurts our feelings. If someone that we know and we think is jealous of us or does not like us says we are fat in front of the person that we are attracted to, it hurts, and it affects our behavior.

Instead of thinking about modifying our behavior, we have to think about reacting to it. If you think about this for a moment, you will notice that a great deal of American culture reacts badly to criticism, even when it is constructive or about things that are bad. We live in a society now where saying to someone, "I am worried about your health," can be considered offensive. I talk about this a great deal because I am overweight and your waistline is one of the best predictors of how long you will live; the bigger your waist, the shorter your life. Study after study confirm this, and yet saying to someone, "I love you, and I want to spend fifty years with you, not thirty. You have to lose weight because I want to spend more time together," can be interpreted through the lens of an attack. People therefore do not alter their behavior; they just do not see the constructive intention.

2. Become more mindful

Mindfulness is a powerful word; it is a bit of a trendy word at the moment, which means we hear it so much that sometimes we ignore it to block out the noise. Being mindful simply means living in the moment; not regretting the past or worrying about the future. Have you ever found yourself doing something and you got so distracted thinking about the future that you missed what was happening the moment? We cannot change the past or the future; we can only change the "right now."

The more you live in the moment, the more in touch with reality and the universe you become. Every second in your life is one second worth of thinking available. The more you spend it thinking about the past or the future, the more you throw it away. You are wasting a finite resource.

This is not to say that nothing will ever happen that worries you. I had a phone call last week that I was very worried about. This is why the principal's examples were on my mind. Someone with a great deal of power over my business sent me an email saying they wanted to talk on the phone, and for no reason, I was a little bit nervous.

I was thinking my mind what if something bad happens. Every time I had talked to this person before (which was three times), they had done something very good from a business point of view, and it had been very good for me. I love talking to this person – something good always happens – but I was a little bit nervous because a little thought snuck into the back of my head that said, "Maybe you are in trouble." This was not grounded in reality, but it still happens sometimes.

I recognized the thought, and I said to myself, "There is nothing I can do by worrying about it." And I pushed the thought aside. It was not easy, but it was the right thing to do, and when I talked to that person, everything was fine. In fact, he had amazing news for me; better news than my wildest expectation. Live in the moment; we all have things in our past that we regret and mistakes we have made, but worrying about them now does not change them.

When you get trapped thinking about the past, all you are doing is thinking, and you are not in control. You end up in a loop. We see people who live lives in reference to an event that happened ten, twenty, thirty or fifty years ago, and they always talk about it, whether it's a positive or a negative event. We need to break through that and say, "I am just going to focus on the part of the universe I can affect, which is the right now."

3. Learn to create quietness

Thoughts are noisy, and our heads can get filled with distractions. Depending on who you are, you can think about between five and seven things at a time. Only very skilled people could push that number a little bit higher. Study after study showed that multitasking leads to greater efficiency, but the panacea of ten years ago has now become a mistake. We no longer think of multitasking as the panacea of success; we now believe in focus again.

Some of us can work on one task and be distracted by three or four different things, and if we get more and more thoughts going, we can end up with six distractions, and the only important thing we are doing is sometimes the slot that gets knocked out. That is where you lose focus on what you are doing.

It is like when you read a book, and you get to the bottom of a page and go, "I have no idea what just happened," and you have to re-read it. That is a waste of your time; if you have to re-read a page of this book, that is a dead giveaway that there is a problem in your focus and in your thought life.

There are many practices that can help you get focus and take control of your thought life: yoga, meditation, and exercise are all tools that I use very much. Anything artistic, such as coloring books, is a very powerful tool as well. When you use a coloring book correctly, it acts as a focus-building tool. You want to use techniques that are hard enough to take up all of your mental bandwidths.

When you cannot think about anything else, it forces you to live in the moment. I can color anything with crayons mindlessly, but if I start using paints and pencils and very complicated designs all at once, suddenly all seven slots are filled up, and there is no room for those negative extraneous thoughts. This helps me practice both physical activity and mindfulness while controlling those extraneous thoughts and having a firm and guarded thought life. There are many ways we can train ourselves to strengthen the walls of our thoughts.

4. Fight against bad thoughts

If you have a negative, distracting thought, or if you have a thought that you are thinking over and over again, you can fight against it; you can say to your mind, "I reject this thought."

There is one exercise that one of my neuro-linguistic

programming (NLP) coaches taught me once; it helps me to deal with extraneous thoughts. Sometimes, when you have a thought, that is your mind warning you of an old danger. Our minds are still trained to warn us of dangers that no longer exist; these are atavistic thoughts. These are responses that mattered a long time ago and are no longer relevant.

For example, thousands of years ago, when we were tribal societies, in every group of two hundred people or less, if you walked up and talked to the chief's wife without knowing her, you might get hit in the head with a rock. This is why men are often afraid to walk up and talk to women in a bar; we have an atavistic fear. Back then, this fear was reasonable, but in my thirty-six years on this planet, I have yet to see someone hit in the head with a rock in a bar for talking to the wrong person.

We no longer need that training, but it still exists in our mind. A way to deal with these atavistic thoughts is to say to your mind or to the fear, "Thank you mind for pointing out this danger to me; I have heard the information and absorbed it, you do not need to push that button anymore. You can stop ringing the alarm bell; I am at battle stations." It is time to react to the information and prepare to deal with this information, rather than just be caught in a state of emergency.

5. Use your Law of Attraction Journal

Write down every thought that is distressing you. Whenever you have an extraneous thought or a thought is beginning to take dominion in the back of your mind, and the first several techniques are not working, write down exactly what that thought is. What you can do is create a little predictive analysis tool.

Every time you worry, write it down, and at the end of the week, if the worry never happened, cross it out with an X; if it did happen, circle it. At the end of the week, you will see more Xs than circles. What you will discover is that you are a terrible predictor of the future; everyone is. Study after study confirmed we are terrible at worrying about the future because we predict and fear the wrong things.

Write down what is worrying you; seeing it on paper might help you realize that it is not that big of a deal. It is when our thoughts are undefined and fluid in our minds that they are so powerful and grow out of control. If we write them down, then we limit them. Every time you fight a thought in the real world, you have a massive advantage. Worry cannot exist outside of your body; it is allergic to oxygen. It cannot survive in the universe.

6. Calm and slow down your mind

There are many techniques for mental relaxation, from yoga to mantras, meditation, and exercise. I implement many of these throughout my life every single day. I practice yoga nearly every single day, both because it requires all of my focus and helps to calm my mind, and because I enjoy the exercise; it works every muscle in my body.

When things are stressful, you can use a technique like anchoring, which is where you attach a specific thought or emotion to a specific behavior. For instance, you touch your pinky finger on your right hand, and it reminds you of a relaxed state. You can develop lots of different techniques; they are all designed to help relax your mind, and we can find the one that is right for you.

7. Replace bad thoughts with good ones

Sometimes, telling a bad thought go away is not enough. Remember you only have five to seven thoughts lots to fill up the slots; the bad ones have to go. One of the ways that I like to do this is I have a list that I keep with me of every accomplishment and every good thing that happened in my life. When I have bad thoughts, I pull it out and think my way through all those things.

As you work your way through the list, you keep pushing that negative thought out until you do not remember what it was and it disappears. This is a very powerful technique that combines distraction with replacement.

Reflection Questions

Please complete these reflection questions in your Law of Attraction Journal.

1. Have you ever heard of any of these methods or techniques before? Have you ever tried them? If you have, what was a result? If you have not ever tried them, why not?

2. If you did try these techniques in the past, how helpful did you find them? What was your experience?

3. What would your life be like if you had total control over your thought life? What would your life be like if you never had another negative thought ever again?

Exercise

Take one of the seven techniques from above and try it out for the next day. Just choose one, and every time you have a negative thought you need to take dominion over, use that technique.

After one day, or if you really want to push yourself, after a week, break open your Law of Attraction Journal and write down your answers to the following questions.

1. Did the technique work? If it did not, do you think it might work better when you have more practice? Why or why not?

2. Did you find the experience of using your technique empowering? Do you feel better about your ability to control your own thoughts now? Has your conference been boosted?

3. Which of the other methods and techniques do you want to try next? Why?

4

MINDFULNESS

I would like to share with you some more techniques you can use to improve your mindfulness. These are all techniques and strategies you can employ to help you stay focused in the moment.

1. Walking. Walking is interesting because we have done it for so long it becomes routine and memory. My son still is learning to walk. He is sixteen months old and is pretty good at walking, but if he gets distracted, he will fall. He still has to actively focus on walking to do it well, and sometimes he walks in different ways. Sometimes he walks on the heels of his foot, sometimes on his toes. Sometimes he uses a bit of a shuffle. He hasn't locked in his gait yet.

You can do the exact same thing; you can walk slowly and think about every single part of the process. When was the last time you thought about whether your heel or your toe touches the ground first? How does your knee react and bend? How does the ground feel, and how does your body react? Feel your muscles twitching and your tendons pulling. Focus on the act of walking. You do not have to walk fast. A great way to start this technique is to reverse your walking. Most people in the West walk heel first, so practice walking toe first. To take each step, you touch the ground with the ball of your foot, and then you lower your heel.

I am doing it right now; it feels very unnatural, and it requires all of my focus. I cannot focus on anything else while I am doing this.

2. Body awareness. If you don't feel like going for a walk, you can lie down on your bed or your couch, close your eyes and practice body awareness.

Try to listen and feel for your heart. Listen to each breath going in and out. Feel every piece of your skin from your feet all the way to the top your head. This is a common meditation technique, and you can find plenty of whole body meditations that walk you through each step of the process. They talk you through feeling your toes, the bottom your foot, then the top of your foot and so on. You can listen to a ten-minute meditation or thirty minutes, depending on how much time you have, and learn to become aware of your body.

When was the last time you thought about your breathing? How often do you breathe through your mouth versus your nose, and how many breaths do you take per minute? Most of us do not think about these things anymore; we are born with the ability to breathe. That takes us to number three.

3. Focus deeply on your breath cycle. Breath in and feel it flowing through your nose, down into your lungs. Hold the breath for a second and slowly release it. Work on lengthening each breath.

The secret of each of these techniques is the same as the secret for coloring books. It is taking a simple process and making it more complicated so that it requires all of our mental bandwidth. Practice breathing and think about the air coming into your nose and your body. Feel your diaphragm going out and squeezing back in. Try to lengthen each breath so that it lasts three seconds, then five seconds, and then seven seconds, and when you breathe out, make it last five seconds, then six seconds, and then nine seconds.

The longer your breaths take, the more focus they require. You can strengthen your lungs while you become more mindful.

4. Meditation. Any form of meditation is specifically designed to help you improve mindfulness. When you are meditating, you are completely and totally focused on one thing.

Any type of meditation will do, whether you are repeating a mantra or listening to a guided meditation, or even if you just listen to relaxing music and try to empty your mind. All of these techniques work; they are all about emptying your mind of the garbage and resetting it so when you start thinking again you feel a bit more in control and you can choose which things you focus on.

Take any of these techniques and slowly increase its complexity until you max out your mental bandwidth.

Reflection Questions

Choose at least three of these questions to answer in your Law of Attraction Journal.

1. How mindful do you think you have been in the past?
2. What do you think your level of mindfulness is right now? Do you tend to worry about the past and the future? Or are you good at living completely in the present moment?
3. How do you feel that improved mindfulness will affect your wisdom?
4. How can improving mindfulness affect your happiness?
5. Which of the methods from the chapter and from the previous mindfulness section do you plan to try? Why did you choose them?

5
THE VITAL SIGNIFICANCE OF GRATITUDE AND POSITIVE THINKING

To truly harness the power of the law of attraction, you must begin by cultivating a sense of gratitude. Many people struggle to see the correlation, so let me tie these two things together for you. When you do something for someone and they are grateful, it makes you want to do something for them again. If the universe does something nice for you, and you don't respond without gratitude, then the universe is going to go, "I am not wasting my time; this person does not appreciate it."

We are more likely to spend time to get gifts for and invest in people who show gratitude. This is why people who fail to show gratitude often get stuck in life. They cannot move to the next level because they are so busy seeing the glass half-empty. They begin to think that the world is against them, and they do not notice that they are living in a prison of their own making. If you have the choice of giving one Christmas present, who would you choose? The person who is grateful and says thank you or the person who takes it and goes "Oh, alright," and shrugs? We prefer to give things to people who are grateful.

Additionally, gratitude is a critical bulwark in preventing us from entering negative mental cycles. People who are not grateful for the small things become very negative; they become bitter and unpleasant to be around. They develop self-fulfilling prophecies by saying, "The whole world is against me." The whole world was not against you until you said that. I once had a business partner who emailed every single person we were working with saying (and I quote) that our project had "one foot in the grave." With one email, he killed our business.

You can create and affect the universe with negative thoughts and words just as much as with positive thoughts and words. Remember that the focus of your mental energy affects the universe. The first half of the law attraction says that if you think about something and focus on it enough, with the right thinking and the right mindset, it will come to you. But there is a negative corollary that most people ignore, and that is when you have negative thoughts you bring negative things into your life.

The more you expect bad things to happen, the more they will happen. This is not a mystical or metaphysical principle; it is a principle of perception. Think about what we talked about in the last chapter; when you are in a negative state of mind, you interpret everything negatively. It is your interpretation that leads to a cycle of more and more negative results. We want to reverse that.

If you live in a Western nation, you are already in the top one percent of people on the planet. I live in a country that has Third World living conditions, where people die of starvation, and most families have large numbers of children because they expect one or two out of every five to not make it to adulthood. My wife has fought multiple wild animals for her life. When you hear that sentence, what you are imagining in the West is fighting someone's poodle chasing you. I am talking about a wild animal you are fighting to survive: one of you is going to live, and one of you is going to die. I am talking as young as six years old. She had a sibling killed by a snake in her crib. These are not things we experience in the West.

Homeless people in America have it far better than most people where I live. We are so used to our lives that we do not notice and we do not care about other people. Most of the things that people complain about in the West are things that people where I live never even think about. Every day, my wife and children are grateful we have air conditioning because my wife spent eighteen years of her life without even knowing what it was. She is grateful every day that she and her children are not hungry because she knows what it is like to grow hungry – to wonder if you can last long enough until you find your next meal.

No matter how bad you think you have it, there is someone who's got it worse, and therefore you should be grateful that you are doing better than them. It can be hard to shift your personality to simply become more grateful. How can you do that? Let me take you through some steps along that process so we can implement this concept and you can shift in a better direction.

Tips for Cultivating a Greater Sense of Gratitude

Allow me to share with you ten different techniques that you can use to improve your sense of gratitude, take more control of your thought life, and become what I can only describe as a better person. We talked about removing the negative thoughts; now we want to replace negativity with positivity. The more positive energy we can plant into your mind, the more good things will come to you magnetically.

1. Think about people who have done nice things for you. You can rekindle old relationships and message people to let them know they did things that altered the course of your life or that you remember them. There are certain moments in my life that were very significant for me but are totally forgetful for the other person. For instance, the first day I studied my popular friend and decided I would model him to learn how to become popular and make friends changed my life.

He has no idea whatsoever, and that is okay. Remembering those moments and being grateful for what happened is about you; it is not about the other person. The person does not need to acknowledge your gratitude. You can sit down and make a list of all the things that people have done for that made your life better. Stop focusing on the negative; focus on the positive.

2. Smile, even when you do not feel like it. Physiology and psychology are intertwined; they are the yin and yang of your body and mind. Just as a bad mood can affect your face and cause you to frown, if you smile and hold your smile, it will force your mood positive. Your body and your mind cannot be at war with each other. One emotion will always win.

Rather than fighting sadness or any mental problem in your mind, fight them in your body. Stand in front of the mirror and hold a smile on your face. Laugh, no matter what. If you laugh when something is not funny, and you keep laughing, eventually you will think it is funny. You can force your mood to follow your body.

3. Stop comparing yourself to other people. The only person you should ever compare yourself to is yourself yesterday – the past version of you. If you can do a little bit better today than you did yesterday, you should feel good about yourself and reward that. If you are doing worse than you did yesterday, you can say, "I've got to try harder," and give yourself some motivation. Anything beyond that is ridiculous.

You do not know what other people go through. One of the people I work with is far more successful than me. He works harder than me, he is more analytical than me, and it took a different approach to building his business compared to mine. He just had a tragedy in his life that I would not wish on my worst enemy, and most people do not know about it. We keep the bad things in our life private.

Do not compare yourself to other people because you have no idea what it is like to walk in their shoes. I do not care if they're rich, famous, or beautiful; everyone has something. Be careful what you wish for. The worst thing that could happen is for you to get it and discover that the bad stuff in their life is something that you cannot handle.

I am already trained and have the experience to deal with my own negative problems; I do not want to try and deal with anyone else's. With each of my struggles in every area of life, I am trying to improve. It is okay to compare yourself to other people as a form of motivation, but I do not compare myself to someone else and say, "I am not good enough." That is not what you want to do.

It is okay to have people that you look up to and want to model what they are doing, but you should not compare yourself to them and hold yourself to that standard because it is impossible. You only know half the story.

4. Remind yourself to be grateful for what you have. It is easy to say, but how do you implement it? Great question. Make a list of all the good things in your life; everything positive, and everything that other people do not have. You have somewhere to live? Winning. Have you eaten in the last twenty-four hours? Winning. You have air conditioning in the summer and heat in the winter? You have a job? A car? Is anybody actively trying to hurt you right now? Is there someone trying to murder you? Or burn your village down? Guess what, you are in the top one percent.

There are a lot of people who cannot answer those questions the way you just did. Earlier this year, my wife and I went through a miscarriage; it sucked. I have never fought harder for anything in my life than I did for our child. Flying all over the country, taking boats, and doing whatever it took to see the best specialist and get the best care for my wife. We finally saw the specialists, who went through everything and said we were okay; everything was fine. Two days later, we lost the child. We suffered double, but it could be worse. Other people got worse things. I am grateful for the children that we already have and the other children coming down the pipeline in my family. We are not done having children by a long shot.

Focus on the good things, not the bad ones. I do not want you to think that nothing bad happens to me and that the only reason I am happy is that I am rich and living on a tropical island. I recently had a fight with my father, and we did not speak for six weeks. That is not that bad on the spectrum of bad things, and yet some people have a disagreement with a family member and make it the centerpiece of their entire existence; it turns them into a bitter monster.

Make a list of positive things and continually add items to it; if you sit down and focus, you will discover that the number of good things in your life is astounding.

5. You can go one step beyond your list and create a Gratitude Journal. Every week or every day, write down good things that happen to you. There is a section in the Law of Attraction Journal, or you can create a section in your own Journal where you just write down good things that happened during the week – someone smiled at me, someone held the door for me, I had a lovely dinner tonight and so on. Keeping a journal creates a trend; it trains you to focus on the positive, and it moves you from pessimism to optimism through a very simple practice. It helps you to remember the right events each day.

6. Work on your mindfulness. We are going to circle back to the mindfulness principal over and over again because it is so powerful. When you are living in the moment, you are not distracted by the past or the future. When something good happens, you will notice it right then.

7. Look for the silver lining. Earlier this year, I thought I was going blind; I went through some serious problems with my eyes. When I finally flew to a big city to see an eye doctor, he told me nothing was wrong, and yet I still suffer with my eyes every day. If I look at a computer screen for too long, my eyes hurt. I am a writer; my job is to sit in front of the

computer and write, edit, create, and research. I suddenly found I could not use the primary tool for my entire career.

Between that and those days where I thought I was going blind before I saw the eye doctor, I went through a great deal of emotional turmoil. It was not an easy time for me. I started planning on how I could change my business so I could continue to take care of my family even if I completely lost my vision. I can only spend a certain number of hours at the computer (and I say a certain number because I do not know, every day my eyes just start to hurt after a certain amount time), and if I stare too long, the pain will get to the point that I have to lie on my bed wearing an eye mask for the next day or day and half. My eyes hurt so much I cannot use them at all.

I learned not to push myself, and sometimes I can work for an hour, sometimes I can work for five hours. That is what I call a long day. When you are a writer and your work is all computer-based, a five-hour day is not nearly enough. I could focus on my limitation, but instead, I am grateful that I am not going blind, and the silver lining is that I changed my business model to something better.

I now write every single thing via dictation; not because I'm a fancy man, not because I am super rich, not because I want to show off my affluence, but because I have no choice as a result of a medical condition. To write this book, I am dictating it, while I am standing on the beach at sunset in paradise. The result of my eye pain and my medical trauma is that I spend more time outside.

Additionally, instead of sitting in front of the computer, I pace back and forth on my dock, and I walk seven to ten kilometers a day while I write. All my friends with their fancy treadmill desks have nothing on me. As someone who is overweight, I have to exercise more and more as I get older to stay ahead of the curve and to stay ahead of my challenge. When I think about my eye problems, I mostly talk about the benefits.

After going through something so scary, I now get more exercise and work faster because I transcribe and dictate faster than I can write by hand, and I spend more time outside and with my children. All benefits; all silver lining to something that initially scared me.

8. Be happy when things go well for the people around you. It is easy to think of good fortune and success as a zero-sum game, where other people's success pushes us down, but it is not a competition. Every time I see someone who is in the same industry as me, doing similar things but doing better in some area, my first thought is alliance. How can I partner with this person? How can we do things to help each other? A rising tide raises all ships.

When my friends have great success, I am happy for them. There is a tendency in us to have a twinge of jealousy, "Why did she get the job when I work so much harder?" Then it goes a step further; we think stuff like "She probably got it because of her looks." Then we go even beyond that, and maybe we say, "She must have done something with the boss to get that promotion. We have all had that thought, and it is a common theme in loads of movies and television shows for a reason.

You end up poisoning your view of the world. Instead, be happy for other people. Even if that is how she got the promotion, so what? Do not let other people's experiences pull you down; be happy for them. I was doing better than certain friends of mine three years ago, and now they make one hundred or one thousand times more money than me per month. Of course, there is a part of me that has a twinge of jealousy or desire to catch up to them and hit that number too. I have to actively resist that and instead be happy for them.

I am happy when my friends have success, and I am happy when my friends achieve their goals and their dreams come true.

9. Appreciate the little things. Every day, there are thousands of little things that go right for you. You get to work without your car crashing, without your car running out of gas, without going past a tornado – that is a pretty big win. You go to your favorite restaurant, and they have your favorite food, which is pretty good. You go to buy something that is on sale, which is pretty good. Things can go your way all the time without you noticing. Focus on those. Keeping your Gratitude Journal will help you train your mind and think about the good things that happen throughout the day. We want to be proactive as we develop this process.

10. Spend more time doing things you enjoy. It is hard to be grateful and happy when everything you do is something you hate. Find hobbies and cultivate habits and patterns that are things you enjoy. I fill my day with stuff that I like to do. I like writing, which is why I write so much. I am not prolific out of necessity; I am prolific out of desire and passion for what I do. In addition to that, I make sure that I fill my day with fun little things, and I found sports and athletic things that I enjoy that also keep me healthy.

Earlier today, I was in the kayak with my kids, then my wife joined us. The kayak was full, and I was the only one with the paddle. My shoulders are on fire right now, but I enjoyed it. We had an adventure. I have been swimming twice today with the kids. I have even been playing video games for thirty minutes; it is a nice day. Add more and more little things to your days and weeks so you can be in a perpetual state of happiness and gratitude.

Reflection Questions

You should complete at least five of these questions. Write your answers in your Law of Attraction Journal.

1. Have you ever thought of gratitude in this way before? Did you realize that gratitude could actually lead to happiness?

2. Give an overview of what you have learned in this chapter. Do you feel that your new knowledge will benefit you? Why or why not?

3. How difficult do you think you will find it to put our ideas about gratitude into practice?

4. Which of the methods we described above do you think will be most helpful to you? Which of them do you plan to try first?

5. Do you know anyone who seems to understand and use the power of gratitude to improve their own lives? Did you realize this before, or have you only come to recognize it by reading this chapter? Explain how you think that this person's life has improved as a result of living their lives in this way.

6. Do you know anyone who could benefit from understanding the power of gratitude in improving the happiness of their lives? Why do you think of this?

7. What little things in your life do you now feel a greater

sense of gratitude for? Why? Why do you think you did not feel grateful for them earlier in your life? How do you feel that that may have negatively affected your level of happiness?

8. Think of one thing from your childhood for which you are especially grateful. Write down all the reasons why you are so grateful for it.

9. Think of one thing from your adolescence for which you are especially grateful. Write down all the reasons why you are so grateful for it.

10. Think of one thing from your life as an adult for which you are especially grateful. Write down all the reasons why you are so grateful for it.

Exercises

Below are four exercises designed to help you cultivate a stronger sense of gratitude. Please complete the exercises that require writing in your Law of Attraction Journal.

1. Go for a peaceful and leisurely walk. While you walk, take care to maintain a high level of mindfulness (living completely in the present, with no thoughts of the past or future). Observe everything around you, and find something to be grateful for in every single thing. For example, you could feel gratitude for the beauty of the songs of birds in the trees, the bright color of the flowers, the cloudless sky, or the feeling of a light drizzle in your hair.

When you get home, write a reflection on your experience in your Law of Attraction Journal.

2. Use your answer to question 8 in the reflection questions for this chapter. That question asked you to think of one thing from your childhood for which you are especially grateful. Answer the questions below on that thing that inspires so much gratitude:

a) Why did you choose this specific thing? Did it immediately come to mind or did you have to reflect for quite a while before you thought of it?

b) What is it about this thing that makes you so grateful? Do you feel that your life today would be different if it had never existed/happened?

c) Has reading this chapter made you think of other elements of your childhood for which you can be grateful that you had never thought of before in a positive light?

3. This is a very challenging exercise for most people, but you can do it! Think of something that you generally think of in a completely negative light and find a reason to be grateful for it. This might take quite a while, but the rewards make the effort worthwhile.

4. Every morning, when you wake up, make a point of thinking of something you can be grateful for on that day. You can write whatever you come up with in the Gratitude Journal we suggested creating earlier. Alternatively, you could record it in your Law of Attraction Journal.

6

CHOOSE TO BE HAPPY!

This is a concept that many of us in the West struggle with. We grow up in a materialistic culture that is built around external validation. We are brought up to believe that we can be happy only when we achieve certain things, and we end up on these perpetual cycles where we are constantly chasing that event that will allow us to be happy. "If I get my dream job, I will be happy; if I get the promotion, I will be happy." But we are never as happy as we think we're going to be.

Study after study has shown that no matter how expensive the purchase, after about two or three weeks with that feeling of euphoria, the happy, victorious feeling disappears. What was new becomes the usual. Buying a new car is fun and exciting; the first time you buy that car and you take it home or you take it out for a spin, it feels wonderful. Then you drive to work, and when someone checks your car out and goes, "Wow, nice new car," it feels really good.

Not only do you have a good feeling of accomplishing a goal, but you also get external validation from other people; of course it feels good. After driving to and from work ten or twenty times over the next week though, it loses its luster. Your car goes from new to familiar, and even though you spent a significant amount of money (or perhaps you are going to spend it over the next several years, paying off the car), that good feeling has disappeared.

This is how people become shopaholics and end up chasing different types of emotional highs. Whether they are adrenaline junkies or anything else, they are always chasing that next experience. Instead, we need to change our mindset; no longer do we need to wait for happiness to come from the outside. Delete this formula from your mind: "I can be happy when...happens." This formula is the death of your happiness. Instead, you can be happy along the way; you can be happy every step of the journey. Happiness should come from within.

When I was a child, there was a cartoon I liked to watch called *Inside Out Boy*. It was a Claymation cartoon that they showed in between episodes of other shows on Nickelodeon. This boy was on the swing one day, and he went so far he did a loop over the swing, which is something every kid dreams about. Then, when he came on the other side, his body was inside out. His organs were on the outside, and he dedicated the rest of his life to grossing out his sisters by eating in front of them.

As someone with three sisters and no brothers, this greatly appealed to me. I was not able to show my organs while I digested, but I certainly enjoyed eating with my mouth open in honor of my hero – much to my sisters' chagrin and disgust.

The reason I bring up *Inside Out Boy* is that he is very visual and it creates a very strong memory. You are going to remember the story forever, and if you go to visit the Law of Attraction page on my website, I found a few clips of *Inside*

Out Boy that you could watch. Watching them will help you remember that happiness should come from the inside, and the same goes for validation.

You can be happy first and then seek other things. We have this idea that you have to suffer along the way, or that the more painful the journey, the greater the reward at the end. That is ridiculous; why not enjoy the journey and enjoy the victory? When my friend taught me this lesson, it was revolutionary for me. It changed how I felt.

One of the greatest impediments to my happiness fell away; the scales disappeared from my eyes. I was not born feeling this way, and I did not learn this lesson until my late twenties, but it is one of the most significant and powerful lessons I have ever learned. I share it with you now because it can change your life. You can make the decision to be happy whenever you want. Remember: you are in control of your emotions. You can make a choice, and you can choose right now.

There may be voices in the back your head that are saying, "Oh, that does not apply to you," or, "You are not good enough." It is time to tell those voices to shut up their mouth. That is why I covered that technique first. You deserve to be happy, and you can be happy every step of the journey. You do not have to suffer to get to the top of the mountain. If one person becomes a millionaire and every day of their life is a nightmare until they make that million, while the other person becomes a millionaire and every day of their life is an absolute dream – they have a family they are in love with and an amazing experience, and every day they wake up the smile on her face – which of those two lives would you rather lead?

My parents taught me, just like everyone else's parents taught them, that adversity and challenge build character.

While that is true, you do not need to work on your character every single day. There is enough adversity out there without building your own. I want you to look in the mirror right now and say, "I deserve to be happy and I am making a stand right now: I am going to choose to be happy because I deserve it."

Choosing Happiness Allows You to Harness the Power of the Law of Attraction

The law of attraction is built around your mental state. When you are in a negative mental state, you repel the universe. I have a very binary personality; I am either very extroverted or very introverted. When I am introverted, I push away strangers, and I do not talk to other people. I try to keep my face looking unfriendly so that people avoid striking up conversations with me. When I am in an extroverted cycle, I am smiling to everyone; I am very open, and more people walk up and talk to me.

When I am in an extroverted state, strangers will walk up to me and ask for directions all the time. When I am in an introverted state, nobody ever asks for directions. In the same way, your positive mindset will attract the positivity of the universe, while a negative mindset will repel it.

One of the ways the universe will make things happen for you is by introducing you to people who can make your dreams come true. The universe can bring you someone who has access to that thing you are looking for. Perhaps your dream is having a specific car, and you run into the person who owns that dealership or who works at that dealership. Just by having this relationship, you could cut five or ten percent off the price of that car. But if you meet this person and you are not in a happy state of mind, your personality will repel them.

Even beyond the idea of attracting or repelling the universe, you can also attract or repel other people. My wife grew up in abject poverty; if you are in a Western country, you will never understand the way she grew up. I certainly do not. Her fears are things that I was never afraid of. I never wondered if I was going to starve to death as a child. I never wondered if animals were going to kill me. I never wondered if I was going to die in a natural disaster.

When I met my wife, the first thing I noticed is that she was the happiest and kindest person I had ever met. Beyond everything else, the number one reason that I married her was her kindness and her happiness in the face of adversity. Her life now is unbelievably different, and her happiness is the sole thing that changed the course of her destiny. Happiness can change your life; it certainly changed hers.

Remember What We Learned About Gratitude!

One of the reasons we covered gratitude in the last chapters is that gratitude makes it easy to be happy. When you think about all the good things that happened earlier today, it is easy to stay happy. I read nearly every review people leave for my books, and people either love me or hate me. When I get a review, people either say, "I hate him; all he does is talk about his life and how good his life is living on an island and swimming every day."

They read that and think it is me bragging or humble-bragging to demonstrate how good my life is, but it is not. It is just me in the act of being grateful for my life. I worked very hard to get here; people do not know the sacrifices I made, but when they do, they understand that I enjoy the simple pleasures, and I want you to approach your life the same way. You should only talk about the good things that happened all day, and I would love to hear that in my Facebook group. I love hearing people's stories, but I want to hear about the good things in your life. I want to hear that you have a bigger house than me, that you have a nicer car than me, that your kids love you and are still part of your life and that you've been married to the same person for fifty years.

Reflection Questions

Choose at least three of these questions and write your answers your Law of Attraction Journal.

1. Do you feel that the lessons you learned in this chapter will help become happier?

2. After completing the chapter, did you feel happier? How much happier did you feel? Were you surprised by this? Why or why not?

3. Can you think of a time in your life when simply choosing to be happy would have improved how you felt and experienced the entire situation? Would it have changed how things turn out in the end? Describe it and explain.

    I can think of certain things that I have done that I regret. I will share a story that I have never shared publicly before. When I was in high school, I went away for the summer every year. I was on the debate teams, and I would go to colleges and study new debate topics and prepare for the new school year.

One summer, when I came back, my mother had cleaned out my entire room. Along the way, she discovered many of my secrets, from my BB gun to a Victoria's Secret catalog that I had hidden five years earlier behind my bed, and a few other things that I do not need to mention here. She cleaned the entire room and reorganized everything in an effort to make it easier for me to come back after being away for seven weeks.

When I came home, I was enraged; my privacy had been violated. I did not see her effort to clean the room and prepare for me. All I saw was a violation of my privacy, and that things were not where I like to keep them. Books were in the wrong place; clothes were disorganized.

If you are a person who cares a great deal about structure, when your shirts are in your shorts' drawer, and your shorts are in your shirts' drawer, you can get a little upset. I responded like a horrible teenager. My parents were displeased. They were about to take me out to the movies to see the movie *The Mask*, starring Jim Carrey, who at the time was one of my favorite actors. It was a movie I had been looking forward to seeing, and my parents said, "You cannot come to the movies with us. Not only that; you are never allowed to watch that movie for the rest of your life!" This was twenty years ago, and I still have not seen that movie.

I reacted emotionally, and I didn't get to see that movie. Instead, I spent hours and hours reorganizing my room, undoing my mother's work and stewing in my own anger. What a waste of an afternoon.

4. Has this chapter already been a revelation for you? Is the

idea that you can choose to be happy something that has never crossed your mind before? Have you ever realized before reading this chapter that you can choose whether or not to be happy?

5. Do you feel empowered by what you have learned so far in this chapter? Why or why not?

Exercises

1. Read a book or watch a movie or an episode of a television show. Focus on one of the characters and brainstorm ways you think their life would improve if they chose to be happy. Are you surprised by how many different ways you can come up with? Why or why not? For this exercise, I recommend choosing a drama rather than a comedy; it is easy to find characters that work with this exercise.

2. If you have issues with self-esteem, does start an I Deserve Happiness Notebook. It can simply be a section in your Law of Attraction Journal; you can start filling out from the back of the book as if it were a new book. You do not have to get a second notebook, but you are certainly welcome to. Every day, write in it affirmations about the fact that you are a wonderful person and deserve happiness. Additionally, write down daily affirmations that you choose to be happy. Every morning, you can get up, open your notebook, and simply write, "Today I choose to be happy." When you come home, and before you go to bed, your final note can be, "Today I chose to be happy."

3. One of the movies that I saw and thought was pretty brilliant (and you know I love talking about books and movies that I have seen) was a movie called Pay It Forward, where a little boy came up with the idea of doing three favors for strangers. Instead of waiting for favors to come to you, put favors into the universe. This ties nicely with the idea of karma – you get back what you put into the world – or simply the golden rule: treat people the way you always want to be treated. And who would not love a favor from a stranger? Of course, the movie goes down a rather dark path, and I do not want to spoil it for you if you have not seen it. It was a little off the track, but I like that core concept. Doing nice things for strangers is a good thing. This is an exercise where you can see your ability to influence the world and affect strangers.

You can simply decide to perform random acts of kindness at different times. When someone in line in front of the grocery store does not have enough change, throw a penny their way and watch the stress disappear from the shoulders. Hold the door for someone. We start with small things, and I want you to see how you can affect other people's emotions with such tiny acts. We all know that misery loves company, but all emotions are contagious. When you put a smile on someone else's face, it is going to make you feel good. In this exercise, not only do you get to see your ability to affect and influence the world, but you also get to feel good while you are doing it – double win.

7

THINKING ABOUT THE UNIVERSE

What do we mean here when we talk about the universe? It does sound a bit metaphysical, and it is easy to get caught up in thinking of the law of attraction like a magic spell. I hope by now you realize that there is a real-world interpretation that is far more powerful and effective.

The universe does not mean something invisible; it does not mean outside of our atmosphere. I am not talking about galaxies and other planets. Your hopes and dreams will not affect the moon. Instead, the universe is the world around you – the world you inhabit. It is everything outside of your skin; it is your roommates, your spouse, your family or friends or coworkers, and even strangers walking down the street. It is the other people and everything else around you.

Through the right thoughts and right actions, you can affect the universe in order to receive that which you most desire. The universe is everything, and this is why sometimes we call it "the source," because it is the source of everything outside of your body. Every breath of air coming into your body comes from the universe; every relationship you have with another person comes from the universe outside your body. If I say "source" instead of "universe," you know what I mean now.

Take some time to brainstorm everything you associate with the word "energy." How does the word energy relate specifically to your mind and spirit?

If it is not clear by now, I would like to reiterate that the way you think affects the world around you. Positive energy attracts positive energy; negative energy attracts negative energy. A way to see this in the real world is to think about who we become friends with. Sarcastic, negative people become friends with other sarcastic, negative people.

Think of the cliques in high school; the group of kids that sit around making fun of everyone else attract themselves to each other, while the kids that are happy all the time attract each other and are a separate group. We do not just have to look at the metaphysical; we can look at the physical. The way this works is that beliefs control thoughts, thoughts control decisions, and decisions control actions.

On a core level, your belief, whether it is positive or negative, will color every single decision you make for the rest of the day. When I was in a negative state of mind, I poorly misinterpreted my mother's effort to make my life a little easier by cleaning my room. Had I been in a positive state of mind, my reaction would have been different, and it would have brought even more goodness into my life.

Before we think about directly affecting the universe with our thoughts and our emotions, we can think about how our thoughts affect our body, our facial expressions, how we talk with people, and how we interpret what other people say. The more you interpret everything through a positive lens, the more you respond in a positive way, and the more positivity will attract itself to you.

Throughout my life, I dated a spectrum of women, and I dated quite a few women that were really mean. When I dated them, I became meaner; they made me a worse person. This is why I had a revelation and realized I have to date someone who is very positive because then I get pulled towards positivity. As much as it seemed like in the last chapter I was talking about how my wife's life changed because now she is with me and she no longer has to worry about many of the challenges she faced when she was younger, she also made my life significantly better. Every day, I am happier because she is in it. She is a magnetic pole pulling me toward happiness every single day.

Exploring Energy

Many people are kind of astounded by the idea that your internal thought life and your internal energy state can affect the universe around you. If someone is happy all the time, from the outside, it may seem like they are just lucky, but this is a common interpretation. Luck is where opportunity meets preparation.

I have friends who had amazing opportunities handed to them in their lives. I am thinking of a specific friend who, for some reason, is always happy. In all of my memories, I cannot ever remember a time where he was not smiling. This is not someone who's got a lot of money or someone with an amazing career, but he had many wonderful opportunities to travel the world (including climbing part of Mount Everest) come his way and into his family mostly because of his unbelievable disposition.

If you look from the outside, your first thought is, "He is happy all the time, so good things happen to him." If we look at the steps in between though, we can see the science, and it no longer seems to be magic. As Arthur C. Clarke stated, "Any sufficiently advanced technology is indistinguishable from magic." In the same way, when we see someone always happy and good things happening to them, we do not see the steps in between; we think it is the magic of happiness. I want to take you one step further.

If you can see the scientific steps, you can see the logic in this process. People want to be around happy people. When I was very unhappy, no one wanted to be around me. Now that I am a very happy person, people want to be around me all the time. The only thing that changed is my internal energy state.

Reflection Questions

Let us think about energy now. Write your answers to these questions in your Law of Attraction Journal.

1. How would you describe your internal energy right now? How positive or negative is it? You could draw a picture or a graph with positive and negative or use a meter diagram or simply give yourself a score between one and ten or a hundred. How do you visualize it and where do you see yourself on that spectrum?
2. Would you say that your energy is more positive now than it was before you picked up this book?
3. Which thoughts or feelings have you had recently that you think might have radiated negative energy to the universe? Remember we do not want to dwell on these; we simply want to observe past behavior and use it as a lesson and a guide to improve our future behavior.

4. What thoughts or feelings have you had recently that radiated positive energy into the universe?

Your Place in the Universe

You probably realize by now that your place in the universe is more significant than you have ever imagined. The fact of the matter is that as far as your life is concerned, you have your own, personal universe! You can determine whether it is positive or negative, depending on the energies you radiate out to the larger universe (the source). Let us think about what you most want from the universe right now. Have you considered which specific things you want the most? You have the chance to do it here.

Think About Your Dreams

1. What is your most precious dream and why do you cherish this one above all others?

2. What dream have you felt is unattainable in the past? You need to change your thinking about whatever the dream is and realize that it is now attainable

3. In what area of your dreams have you experienced the most obstacles in the past?

4. Do you have any dreams specifically related to your personal life? If you do, what are they? Make sure to take the time to think about this and dial in what you wish for.

4. Do you have a specific dream related to your career? If you do, what is it?

5. Do you have any dreams to travel or have other new experiences? If you do, what are those?

You now know that you are significant, and you have the ability to affect the universe through your thoughts, dreams, actions, behaviors, and beliefs. What you say, do, and think matters. You should start to feel a little bit better about yourself because you are pretty important; you matter. You have your own personal universe wrapped around you.

One of the first lessons I teach many people is how powerful we are in affecting the universe. Right now, you are in a movie, and you are the star. You get to choose who has speaking parts in the movie of your life. If you do not talk to someone or if you walk away from someone while they are talking, they are out of the movie. One of my favorite things to joke about in certain movies is where a character walks out of the room and appears to walk out of the movie, and they never come back again.

It is as though, at the end of that scene, they walked too far and left the city the movie was in. That is exactly the power you have over the universe; you get to choose who you talk to and who you interact with. You can determine whether your own personal universe (or movie) is positive or negative, depending on the energy you radiate out into the source.

Think about this question and write down your answer in your Law of Attraction Journal: how has learning how incredibly important you are (and how incredibly important every other individual in the world is) affected or changed your perspective on life? Has it changed your idea about the possibilities of life?

Please take a few moments to reflect on this because it is a pivotal moment in this process.

Exercises

Choose at least three or more of these activities to complete.

1. Draw a picture that illustrates how you now see yourself in relation to the universe. Make sure to convey your new perception of your connection to the universe.
2. Write a creative paragraph on your relationship with the universe. Try to use metaphors and similes where you can.
3. Try to think of a piece of music that expresses your connection to the universe. This can be from any genre (for example, classical, rock, or any other).
4. Write a poem describing your connection to the universe. Please write a paragraph explaining what you were trying to communicate.
5. Write a one-page creative and introspective reflection on how everything in the world and the universe is interconnected.
6. Write a short story about one of your dreams coming true as a result of your positive energy.
7. Create an abstract drawing or painting showing your understanding of the universe and your place in it.
8. Write a poem or a short story about how gratitude can help you send out positive energy into the universe and help your dreams come true.
9. Write a comparison of your previous view of the universe with the one you hold now as a result of your new knowledge. Be creative in your descriptions.
10. Create a collage using pictures you have taken or found. This collage should represent your ideas about the universe and your place within it.

The Meaning of Your Life

The meaning of life and our place in the universe is a question that we have all contemplated at certain moments in our life; it is a big part of who we are. As a person trying to achieve a higher level of self-awareness, this question increases in significance. The more you think about it, the stronger your effect on the law of attraction will become.

Take a moment to think about some ideas concerning the meaning of life. What do you feel your life's meaning is at this point? What do you want to be in the future? Do you feel that the way you are currently living your life is contributing towards the fulfillment of your life's purpose? If not, it's time to start thinking about ways to make some changes. These changes can and should be gradual, but you should still be working towards your goal; this will empower you. As much as we talked earlier about enjoying the journey, sometimes we have to go through a period of challenge to come out the other side.

I was a teacher for ten years, and I was not moving me closer to my life's purpose. It was not moving me down the correct path. I was only affecting a limited number of people in a limited way, and I was not affecting the universe significantly. Now, I affect tens of thousands of people every single day as they read one of my books or blog posts, listen to my podcast episodes or watch one of my videos. My influence on the world has become greater as part of my desire to fulfill my life's purpose.

The transitional period between these two careers was a time of struggle and challenge. It took time to get from point A to point B, but I knew that I was moving closer towards my true purpose in life. What you can learn from the law of attraction is that one of the most important things you need to do is alter your thinking. I would like you to examine your thought processes and mindset and ponder whether they are helping or hindering the eventual realization of your dreams.

To say it in smaller words: are your thoughts helping or hurting you? Are your thoughts making your life better or worse?

8
STRENGTHENING THE MIND

As we have already learned and discussed, in order to accomplish and master part one of the law of attraction, we need to take control of our thought life. How can you go about strengthening your mind? We all know that if you want bigger muscles, you can go to the gym and lift heavy things; your muscles will tear and then get bigger and bigger. But what can you do to exercise and strengthen your mind? In this chapter, we're going to explore different ways to strengthen your mind so that you can improve your level of awareness and truly be in control of your thinking.

Methods for Building Mental Strength

Having an agile and active mind is a result of a conscious decision. In the West, we believe that as you get older, your mind atrophies; this is why we expect older people to become forgetful. We worship youth, and we all try to cling onto it as long as we can, but this is only a Western affectation. In other countries, the elderly are revered.

In Asian cultures, your parents move in with you rather than getting put into a home, and there have been some studies on the differences between aging in these two cultures. In the West, when they do memory studies and mental tests, older people perform poorly. Over time, their mental faculties diminish. In the East, where being elderly is revered, they actually perform better at these tests; their minds are more agile at seventy than they were at twenty.

They continue getting smarter for a longer time. Beliefs can affect your results; expecting to lose your mental faculties can cause you to lose your mental faculties. I would like to take you through twelve different techniques and methods to strengthen your mind and help you stay agile and continue to get stronger with your thinking.

1. Keep your mind active

Find new ways to challenge your mind. You could try puzzles or learn a new craft; becoming artistic can open up that part of your mind. I have an entire book called *Coloring Away Your Depression* which goes into great detail about how you can become very good at art while strengthening your mind using adult coloring books. They are a powerful tool because they provide scaffolding while you improve and develop the skill.

You can also learn to play a musical instrument or a new language. If you are not growing, you are shrinking. Many of my friends and acquaintances, the moment we graduate high school, looked at me and said, "I am never going to read a book ever again." They are dumber now than they were the day we graduated from high school twenty years ago.

When you're not stimulating your brain, you slowly

suffer the results of erosion. Even if you think you are maintaining your mental state, you are not. You can only be improving or decreasing; you cannot maintain a neutral state.

2. Meditate

Meditation is a great technique for strengthening your mind; we are going to cover meditation more extensively in one of the later chapters. It is very effective, and it is built around focusing your mind; it's a great way to combine your body with a mental activity.

3. Read

Reading is amazing because it activates so many different parts of your mind; not only does it activate end-user language centers, but it also activates your imagination, your creativity, and your sense of wonder.

I know movies are entertaining and video games are great; I enjoy both, but I read more than anything else I do. It is my primary form of entertainment. I spend more hours a day reading than all my other hobbies combined.

Think about how much focus reading requires; you cannot read and do something else at the same time. Reading engages all of your mind, and you are pulled into the world of the book.

4. Take part in intense conversations or debates

It is okay to disagree with people and have different beliefs. But what you do not want to do is engage in a debate with someone who is in a deep emotional state of mind.

These days, most people on any side of a major issue have taken an emotional position. This means that no amount of facts can change their mind; everything will be interpreted through their pre-existing beliefs. Instead, you want to find people who understand the argument has a conversational structure; then it is a way of talking to someone and seeking truth, rather than a form of competition.

Unfortunately, many people are not able to understand the word "argument" and think it means "fight." True argument is where two people come together with opposing worldviews and keep sharing information in the hopes of finding common ground or bringing their two worldviews into alignment.

5. Get more physical exercise

Just like with your mind, if you do not use your body, it will wither and get weaker, and that will affect the rest of your system. Your brain depends on the rest of your body to provide chemicals, energy, power, and oxygen. If you do not exercise regularly, you cannot provide enough of these nutrients to your body.

Many people in our culture have replaced exercise with coffee; they depend upon caffeine to start their day. But if you exercised every day, you wouldn't need to worry about being tired all the time. If I go too long without exercising, I get slower, and my mood diminishes.

Our minds and bodies are connected to each other. If your body feels bad, it will make your emotions feel worse, and that will affect everything else. Additionally, when you are exercising, it trains your body to focus. You do not have to go to a gym and do something you hate;

what you can do is pick up a sport, and I absolutely recommend this.

Find a physical sport with a fun element to it. This can be frisbee golf, kayaking, soccer, kickball, dodgeball, or anything you enjoy. You still break a sweat, and that is good.

The good thing about sport is that it requires all your focus. When I play soccer with my neighbors, I have to focus one hundred percent. They are all European, which means they're automatically better at soccer than me (and also, they call it football). If I get distracted or I start thinking about work or a problem in my life, I am going to get hit in the face with a soccer ball. There is no time for that.

Sport is enjoyable and social – you are connecting with other people. It keeps you focused in the moment, it strengthens your mind, and it helps you develop mindfulness.

6. Learn about new ideas

Deliberately set out to learn things you do not already know. If you have a very firm political belief, try to learn why the opposite side disagrees with you – understand how they see the world and look at the world through their eyes. This can be very challenging, especially if you are used to responding emotionally to someone who disagrees with you.

Even much of science has turned from logic to emotion these days; it is hard to talk about some scientific topics without people responding emotionally. But you can separate from that and say, "You know what? I do not like it when people disagree with me, but I want to understand where their beliefs come from, so I am going to learn the history of their beliefs."

One of the biggest topics of our days is global warming, and it is my favorite example because I know it is controversial (and I will not tell you which side of the debate I am on). When I talk about global warming with someone, the first thing I ask them is if they know about the population bomb theory – the theory of overpopulation that was in vogue before global warming.

Number two, I ask them if they are familiar with the term "global cooling." The same guy who wrote the late eighties seminal work on global warming wrote a book thirteen years earlier called *Global Cooling*, stating that we were going to freeze to death because of our effect on the environment. These are core facts; it is not something secret or hidden. On my website, I have links to both books, and they are both still available on Amazon. The guy still makes money selling both books.

This is a fact. If someone responds to it emotionally, I have not said anything yet, have I? All I have said is that two books exist. Then I know that they are trapped in a mental prison of their own making. I know that they have not done any research. Whenever people want to convince me of something, I want to be sure that they know what they are talking about. Most of us regurgitate second or third-hand information, and this is why we are poor decision-makers.

Making a conscious decision always involves researching deeper. If you read about a medical study in a news article, click the link and go to the original medical study. You will be astounded to discover how often those medical studies are misquoted. More than a few times, I discovered that the study's conclusion is the exact opposite of the conclusion of the newspaper or magazine article.

7. Play games that use your brain

Chess, board games, solving puzzles, and even Sudoku are all great examples. Play games that are complicated; if you want to maintain your physical dexterity, play Operation, the game where you have to hold little tweezers and pull up bones and organs out of the body of the patient without getting electrocuted. In the same way, we can play games that use our mind and require focus, thinking, and strategy.

Some games these days are unbelievably complicated. As you know, I put out a couple of board games myself (I work with someone who is an absolute master at designing game mechanics). I am not smart enough to design a game myself from scratch, but I am smart enough to play a game. There are many games out there that are very complicated and require a great deal of study.

Even the game Go (sometimes in the West coast we call it Othello), which seems so simple, is actually the most complicated and difficult game in human existence. In fact, only recently, in the last two years, did a computer artificial intelligence finally defeat a master of that game. There are literally billions of moves in this game.

You can look for other classic Eastern games, like mahjongg; could there be a correlation between the fact that people in the East have stronger minds as they get older and the games they enjoy playing? Worth a try.

Board games are wonderful, and I cannot wait until my children are old enough to play Risk with me. The first time, they will discover that dad always betrays when he plays Risk.

8. Work on improving your general health

Make a conscious decision to eat a healthier diet and pay attention to the things that you introduce into your body. If you just make the decision to not put weird chemicals in your body, you will start to feel way better, and your brain will become stronger.

Here is a simple rule I have: I do not eat anything that was inside of a factory. If a machine made it, I do not eat it. That simple rule will change your health; your blood pressure will lower, your mental agility will improve, and your overall sense of well-being will magnify.

Think about how simple that is. My rule is that I only eat food that is actually food. I do not eat stuff that had chemicals jammed into it or that started out as chemicals they mashed together and now call food. I still eat everything everyone else does – meat, vegetables, fruit, and bread are all fine. But if a machine made it, I get a little more skeptical.

One of the last remnants of my poor diet is soda; as much as I am very good about food, in order to focus I drink half a can of soda at the start of my days. I want to be honest with you here. I do not pound cans all day long, and I rarely finish a whole can, but sometimes I drink between one and two cans of soda throughout the whole day, and it is the last vestige of my poor health.

I am in the middle of conquering that last challenge with my diet because I do not like the chemicals in it, and I do not like how it makes me feel, so I am working on replacing it. I did a lot of research and discovered hot chocolate, and this is what I am transitioning to. Here is the thing: you can buy packets of hot chocolate that come from the factory, and if you look at the ingredients, that list is horrifying. Instead, what I have discovered is a simple recipe with pure ingredients – all things that I can acquire where I live, and that is what I am transitioning to. You can see I am not perfect, and I am willing to admit my flaws. By the time you read this, I will have fully transitioned to hot chocolate.

You can also target specific foods that are good for the mind like tomatoes, pumpkin seeds, blueberries, and fish. Avocado is all good for the mind, and dark chocolate too.

You can look online for brain food, and you can take supplements that specifically target strengthening your mind.

9. Be kind to yourself

If you get caught up in a negative thought loop, or you say bad things to yourself or just think poorly of yourself, it can push you down, and it can make it very hard to strengthen your mind. The last thing you want to do is let the inmates run the asylum; you don't want to let your enemy into your mind. If you have a negative thought in there, inside your walls, it is too late. We do not want to let any spies inside of our castle.

10. Use your imagination

Imagination is a skill; it is something we can improve if we exercise it. Unfortunately, because we are part of a culture that is obsessed with entertainment, we lose our imagination early on. As we get older, we are so used to playing video games and getting external sources of entertainment that we no longer depend upon our imagination to create wonderful universes.

I had a wonderful imagination when I was very young, but it diminished as I got older. As my desire to write fiction increases, I have to strengthen my imagination so I can create new and wonderful universes. I am excited to share those universes with the real world once I complete my life's work and my mission with my non-fiction books.

My daughter is four and has a wonderful imagination; she creates imaginary characters all the time, and I love it. I do everything to encourage it. If she wants to have imaginary friends and create imaginary worlds until she is ten, twenty or thirty, I will continue to encourage it because a strong imagination means a strong mind.

11. Explore new places

I am fascinated by the number of people who know nothing about the city in which they live. Every city has secret stories and locations. Most cities have wonderful parks or pieces of nature you can visit.

I love national parks in America; they are unbelievable, and when you go there, there is no one else around. But most of the time, you can discover the secrets that used to take insider knowledge with a thirty-second Internet search. Hop on the old Internet and type in "ten amazing things" or "top things to do" followed by the name of your city. People are making these lists all the time, and you could discover things you never knew were there.

When you begin to see the world as a place that still has new things left for you to discover, your brain realizes you continue growing, and your brain will continue learning. If you continue learning, exploring, and implementing all of these other techniques, your brain will stay in learning mode just like any other part of your body. We can activate different parts of the brain with different activities; imagination, exploration, and your sense of wonder are critical to mental growth and mental strengthening.

12. Invest time in developing your sense of self-awareness

We have talked about this before, but I am going to cover it again because it is critical. Think about what you are thinking about. Go one level deeper; when you are doing something because you are mad, think, "I am doing this because I am mad."

Try to become aware of your thoughts and of what is happening; become an active participant. Instead of thinking of your thoughts as a movie, think of them as a video game. You have a remote control in your hands, and you can affect things; you can pause the game.

I would love to say that I am perfect at this, but it is an area again where I am continuing to grow just like you. Getting better at your thought life and being aware of your thoughts is the first step on the path to altering them.

Sometimes, when I am upset or stressed out, I might say things to my wife or children and one moment later go back and say, "I am sorry, I was not mad at you. I just got bad news from my family, and it distracted me." Because I try to practice awareness, I have to externalize it. The first step on the path to altering your mental patterns is becoming aware of them.

Reflection Questions

Write your answers to these reflection questions in your Law of Attraction Journal.

1. How often do you set about learning something new? How could you do this more often?
2. Have you ever tried meditation? If you have, what did you think of it?

3. How much of a reader are you? How often do you read? What do you most enjoy reading?

4. Do you enjoy debating issues with other people? Why or why not?

5. How often do you exercise? How could you go about boosting your level of exercise per week?

6. How often do you eat each of the brain-healthy foods we discussed earlier?

7. Do you think you are generally kind to yourself? Why or why not? Are you too hard on yourself?

8. How often do you use your imagination? Do you currently consider yourself an imaginative person?

9. How self-aware would you say you currently are? Make sure to explain your answer.

10. What do you think you could do to improve your level of self-awareness?

Exercises

You should choose at least five of the exercises below to complete in your Law of Attraction Journal. One of these should be exercise 9 (on improving self-awareness). The more you complete, the more you will learn!

1. Decide on something new that you want to learn. This can be something big, like a language or musical instrument, or something smaller. After at least one week of devoting a significant amount of time to this endeavor, answer the questions below:

a) Do you feel more mentally alert than you did before starting this project?

b) Do you feel boosted self-esteem and a feeling of self-efficacy (effectiveness)?

c) Do you feel greater faith in your ability to learn new things?

d) Do you feel more excited about life in general?

2. Go for a leisurely walk of at least ten full minutes, preferably somewhere with natural beauty, such as a park. While you walk, remain consistently aware of all the information being received by all five of your senses (sight, smell, touch, hearing, and taste) and remain aware of every physical movement, feeling, and sound involved with your breathing. Once you have finished this walking meditation, reflect on the following questions:

a) How much more centered do you feel now, in comparison to before you started your walk?

b) How much more relaxed do you feel now? How does that state of relaxation manifest itself in your body (for example, in the speed of your breathing and in your heart rate)?

c) Do you feel a greater sense of clarity to your thinking? Explain why or why not?

d) Do you feel a generally greater sense of control over your own life? Explain why or why not?

3. If you are not already much of a reader, this exercise will be very helpful to you. In this exercise, you will set out on a quest to find some book genres that will interest you. Examples of genres include fiction (which includes such subgenres such as classic fiction, science fiction, mystery, and so on), non-fiction, biography, graphic novels, New Age, and self-help.

In order to get started on finding these genres, answer the following questions:

a) What kinds of books have you read in the past? What genres were they?

b) Which of the books and genres you listed in question 1 did you enjoy? Which didn't you enjoy?

c) What book genres have you never tried to read before? Which of these interests you?

4. Think of some ways to boost your exercise routine. You can start this process by answering the questions listed below.

a) How many hours a week do you currently exercise? You can include the time you spend walking from place to place, taking the stairs, and other such everyday activities.

b) How many hours a week do you think you should exercise? What obstacles do you face in making this happen? How can you eliminate or overcome these obstacles?

c) How many hours total per week do you want to exercise? What do you plan to do in order to make this happen?

5. Do a little bit of research and compile a list of games that you would enjoy playing with family and friends. Such games can be card games, challenging board games, chess, checkers, and so on. For each game, you find that interests you, take some time to evaluate whether it will challenge you mentally. Once you have found some games you think will be helpful, set up some time with family and friends to play!

6. Take another look at the list of brain-healthy foods we went over earlier in this chapter. Once you have done this, please answer the questions below.

   a) How many of these foods are currently a part of your diet? For each food that does play a part in your current diet, evaluate whether it is a significant part.

   b) Think of ways you can incorporate each of the brain-healthy foods into your diet. Do some research to find delicious recipes and make sure to save them or write them down somewhere you will remember.

7. Think of a way to treat yourself. Why? Well, quite simply because you're an amazing person! In order to think of the perfect treat, think about the questions below.

   a) What is something within your budget (or that is a slight splurge) that you have wanted for a long time?

   b) What is something that would make you feel lucky or provide a sense of luxury?

8. In this exercise, you will practice using your imagination. After childhood, many of us get completely out of practice with this. Perhaps you hardly ever, or never, use your imagination. If that is the case, you need to make a change now! Your imagination is one of the most precious things you have, and it deserves to be utilized and developed.

   a) Completely relax and use your imagination to visualize your ideal vacation. Try to imagine every aspect of the vacation, from the point of view of all five senses (sight, hearing, smell, taste, and touch).

   b) What is your most cherished dream? Once you have decided on that, imagine it happening (and, as you did in the first part of the exercise, make sure to engage all five senses).

9. As we mentioned earlier, self-awareness is the ability to truly understand one's own thoughts, feelings, and motivations. As you can easily imagine, good self-awareness is critically important in making full use of the law of attraction.

One of the most useful things you can do to become more self-aware is to become an observer of your own thoughts. What does this mean? This means to learn to objectively observe your thoughts, rather than only emotionally engage with them. And even more importantly, it means to realize that you are not your thoughts. Just because a thought comes into your mind doesn't mean you have to pay any attention to it or engage with it in any way. If the thought is unwanted, simply let it pass through out of your mind.

Below are some simple techniques you can use in order to cultivate the ability to be an observer of your thoughts, as described above.

a) Learn to enjoy and harness the power of solitude. Silent solitude is the most useful state for cultivating greater self-awareness. If you don't yet enjoy spending time alone, start small and work up your time gradually.

b) Write a section of your autobiography. This exercise can be especially useful if you choose a part of your life that was particularly difficult.

c) Start keeping a personal daily journal. Daily journal writing will help you better understand your own thoughts, feelings, and motivations.

9

MEDITATION

As we discussed throughout this book, meditation is one of the most powerful and effective ways to strengthen your mind. It is a way not only to only push away negative thoughts, but also reset our mental palate and cleanse our thoughts. It puts us in a state where we are not thinking about anything, allowing us to tackle a new project or endeavor with absolute focus. This allows you to fill more of your focus and thinking slots with right thinking, built around your real target.

In this chapter, we are going to go into more detail about the process of meditation, so you can stick a toe in the water and see if one of these meditation techniques is the right one for you. Meditation is not necessary for everyone, and you may find that you prefer to exercise or do something artistic in order to cleanse your mind. I find meditation, yoga, surfing, and using my coloring books the most effective tools and techniques for me to relax my mind while strengthening it.

Before we start, answer the following questions in your Law of Attraction Journal:

1. How much you know about meditation? Have you tried meditation before?

2. What do you hope to achieve through meditation? Are you excited about trying it?

3. Do you have any pre-existing beliefs about meditation – perhaps you believe that it is an overly religious activity and that makes you more or less interested?

4. Do you have any preconceptions about meditation or expectations on whether it will or will not work for you? Why?

Meditation for Beginners

Most people assume that to meditate you have to sit in a very specific position, hold your hands in a specific position, and repeat the same phrase over and over again. We have seen this meditation pose in lots of movies, cartoons, and television shows, but in fact, you can meditate in any position you like.

You will discover, as you master this process, that certain positions work better for you than others. Some people are better at standing meditation, while some need to sit in a chair and some like to sit on the floor in the lotus position. All of these are absolutely fine, and I am going to share with you a few of the different positions you can choose from.

Whether you are sitting on the ground or in a chair, you want to make sure that you lock in a perfect posture. Whether or not you believe in patterns of energy through your body and maintaining your chi flow, we want to be sure that your nerves, bones, and ligaments are in alignment. Sit up straight when you meditate; this will strengthen your back.

We already know that your physiology affects your

psychology; when you are hunched over, it lowers your self-confidence. When you sit up straight, you feel more assured. When you can stand properly, you look more confident, you feel more confident, and it is better for your health. As someone who hunched for a very long time, I know a thing or two about back pain, and we certainly do not want your back to hurt while you are meditating.

At first, when you begin to dabble with meditation, just trying to sit up straight will take all your attention; you may find that you can only sit up straight for three or four minutes, and that is okay. I am a big believer of getting multiple benefits from each activity; in this case, while you strengthen your mind, you are also strengthening your body.

If you are sitting in a chair, again, make sure you maintain perfect posture; make sure that your feet can reach the floor easily. Sometimes, we use chairs that are too high or too low. I have an adjustable desk chair, and when the kids or my wife use it, it gets readjusted, so when I sit back in it does not feel right. If it is two inches too high or too low, I do not feel that perfect balance. If you are sitting in a chair, you want to sit all the way back in the chair; the very bottom of your spine should be curved, which will tip the top of your pelvis forward. Your knees should be higher than your bum, and your feet need to be flat on the ground.

From this position, place your hands on your lap, palms up, and you can begin to meditate. If you are sitting on the floor, you want to sit cross-legged. There are different variations on this; sometimes you have a foot on each of your knees – some people can only fit one foot on a knee and the other one below. Just do your best, and over time you will become a little bit more flexible, and you can try some more advanced positions, but sit in a way that is comfortable and allows you to keep a straight back.

You could place your hand palms down or around your knees. You might prefer to place your hands on your lap, palms up, with one hand on top of the other, forming a little basket from your bellybutton. You may even decide to put a hand on top of each knee, which more of what we expect to see.

With standing meditation, you can choose whichever position you like the most; as long as you have a strong and effective posture, everything else will be fine. In order to get your posture right, imagine there is a string going to the top of your head all the way down to the bottom of your feet, and that string should be a straight line.

Just imagine pulling your head up an inch or two, and suddenly your whole body comes into alignment. You can almost feel the vertebrae in your spine elongating. From this position, you can have your hands in front of you, cupped one on top of the other in front of your belly, or have them relaxed at your sides; any hand position that helps you relax is going to work.

If you want to practice before you run, try standing with your back against a flat wall. You want a surface that is totally flat, from your head all the way to the ground, and you can stand with the back of your heels and the back of your head against it. This will help you practice building your posture, and again, the more you do this, the better your back will feel. Over time, you will not need to use that wall anymore. It is okay to use an extra tool to help you as you develop this skill in practice your meditation positions.

The Goal of Meditation

Before I introduce the different meditation position, let us answer a fundamental question: why are we doing this? I want you to go into every activity with your eyes open and understand what we are trying to achieve here.

The goal of meditation is to achieve a state of mindfulness. Although we talk about emptying the mind, that does not mean we leave it like an empty vessel or trash can. What we do is remove the extraneous thoughts that are no longer necessary in the moment. Instead of thinking about what you can have for dinner or wonder if you need to finish an assignment for work or what will be on television tonight, we want to simply think about the "right now."

The goal is to simply be in a state of pure existence, where all you're thinking about is the position of your body, the way you're breathing, and the way your skin feels; you are becoming very aware of the present moment. Although it is called emptying your mind, what you are actually doing is filling your mind with the "right now;" you are putting yourself in a state of absolute focus. The beauty of mindfulness and being focused is that it is pretty relaxing.

All of those little things that you are thinking about right now are causing stress and distraction. They are barriers between you and the universe and between you and your true desires. Thinking too much about what you are going to have for dinner tonight is a waste of mental energy. When you are instead totally focused on the "right now" and in a perfect state of focus, you are using your mind with absolute efficiency. You are not wasting any energy, and it feels good to be at peace with yourself.

When I say "at peace with yourself," I mean silencing all those distractions, negative thoughts, and bad energy that suck up so much of your attention and instead just enjoying being alive.

As a practice, meditation is good for fostering self-discipline. It helps you to achieve a state of mindfulness so that even when you are not meditating, your mind is stronger and more able to stay in the moment. You are developing a very powerful skill: you have an anchor in a physical thing you can do to trigger a state of mindfulness.

When you meditate for the first time, it might take you thirty minutes to empty your mind, and that is okay. The first few times it can be hard, but over time, you will be able to just sit down, relax, and enter a state of pure mindfulness in thirty seconds. It is a very powerful tool. Whenever you are feeling stressed out at work, you can go to the bathroom, relax for a few minutes in a sitting position, and come out totally focused and at peace with yourself.

Your actions and your desires can be in alignment. Meditation is intrinsically connected with the law of attraction because the law of attraction is about being in alignment with yourself so that you can be in alignment with the universe.

In the next section, I am going to go into great detail about the concept of "right action." We are going to talk about the part of the law of attraction that most other books out there ignore. Before your thoughts can affect the universe, all your thoughts within you need to be in alignment.

Many people have multiple thoughts, and you do not want them to disagree with each other. Part of our mind wants to do one thing, and part of our mind wants to do another. Part of us wants to exercise, and part of us wants to eat a piece of pie. We are sending two different signals to our bodies and to the universe. If our body is not sure what our real goal is, how will the universe be sure?

By clearing your mind, you can reset and continually put yourself in a state where all of your thoughts are in alignment. We are only able to think about five to seven things at a time; we want all of those things to be in alignment.

In addition, it is often our subconscious that blocks us from achieving what our conscious is desiring. The more you can enter a state of mindfulness, the more you can notice some of your underlying assumptions and beliefs that may be very well limiting you. If you have a great desire to make more money so you can get ahead of your bills, but at the same time a part of you think that all rich people are bad, you are not in alignment. You have two beliefs that are in a state of disagreement, and you have to reconcile them because your mind is caught in a loop. You have given yourself an unsolvable mathematical equation. You cannot satisfy both your desire to be a good person and your desire to be wealthy until you actively reconcile those in your mind. We have hundreds and thousands of these little beliefs that we do not think about.

Every time you see someone at the gym who is in really good shape, part of you thinks, "I do not like something about them. Look at them showing off; people who are too skinny are too far up their own noses." You had that little passing thought, and it makes your body say, "Uh-oh, if I lose too much weight and start to get to fit, we are going to enter one of those loops. We better make sure that on the way home from the gym, we stop for a little frozen yogurt or ice cream to ensure we do not get too skinny and get into a state where we look in the mirror and do not like what we see."

Your subconscious is protecting you based on the beliefs that you have, even if you have not even realized that they are there. As you meditate and get used to paying attention to all of your thoughts at once, you will start to notice more and more of these as they pass through your mind. You will go, "Wait a minute; this is an unnecessary thought, and it is blocking me. It is sending a mixed signal to my body, and I am going to stop it before it even goes out and sends mixed signals to the universe."

Types of Meditation

There are many different types of meditation. Many of them originated in the Far East, but there are also some new types and techniques that started in the West, as people begin to interpret and build their own meditation practices. I am going to take you through eight of these different styles.

1. Basic breathing meditation

Basic breathing meditation is a great place to start. It simply means focusing in great detail on every aspect of every breath you take. We are so used to breathing that we forget the process. We forget that the first time we learn to breathe, someone had to tell us to do it; the doctor slaps you on the bum to remind you it is time to breathe.

After that, it becomes automatic, and we do not think about it. Many of us have flaws in our breathing process, and if you ever take a singing lesson, you will discover this quickly. Some of us suck our stomach in when we breathe, so we have two forces going against each other. This is a perfect physical parallel to when our thoughts are not in alignment; in this case, our bodies are not in alignment.

When you breathe in, your belly should get bigger, not smaller. You can sit or stand in your meditative position and simply focus on the process of breathing in and breathing out. Most of us breathe through our mouth without thinking about it, even though our noses are a far better and more precise breathing instrument.

Our noses are filled with amazing sensors that determine how much oxygen is in the air and whether there are other chemicals. They block out all unwanted components with those little hairs and everything else in your membranes. When you breathe through your mouth, you bypass that whole security system.

When you are meditating, just try breathing in your nose and out your mouth to create a full circle. If you achieve the highest level, you can breathe in and out at the same time, like some those brilliant master saxophonists that can hold a note for forty-five minutes; that is how they do it. They achieve absolute control over their breathing process.

2. Focused meditation

Some people call this "concentration meditation." We have all seen that scene in a movie where someone gets high and then starts studying their hand: "Wow, look at all those lines on my hand!" It is a little bit funny, but it is also a simple way you could start meditating.

When was the last time you looked at the lines on your hands or thought about the way your hand works? You can study the lines in your hand and focus on many different aspects; think about how your different fingers feel and how they operate. Hands are so complicated you can easily fill all seven of your concentration buckets with different thoughts about different processes within your hand.

The reason I am giving you this hand as an example is that wherever you go, your hand is with you. You do not have to bring an extra object; you can just as easily sit or stand and look at an object on the wall across from you. Just focus on a single dot or square.

With focused meditation, you can focus on different parts of your body, a dot on the wall, or even an image in your mind.

3. Visual objects focus

This is where you choose a specific object that you always use, rather than just a dot on the wall. When I was a kid, and I would go to the wrong TV channel, it would give me a static, and this is called white noise. Many people buy noise machines to help them sleep at night, and they have white noise, pink noise, and other color noises, but they are simply different types of static. You could buy one of these devices if you want something to listen to for focus, but you can also just turn into one of those channels that your TV does not get.

You can also use a candle. Many people find the flickering of the candle hypnotic, and it helps them to get into a focused state where all they are paying attention to is the light of the fire. You could try the same thing with a fire in the fireplace.

Additionally, there are loads of programs now (they come with almost every music player on your computer) that provide a light show where there are lasers and spaceships flying around; they are designed to hypnotize you. These are all great visualizations that suck up your attention without anything actually happening. You are caught in the moment because you are not thinking about what the candle did a second ago or what it is about to do. You are only focusing on the light show in the moment.

4. Mindfulness meditation

You can think of mindfulness meditation as building on top of breathing meditation – going to the next level. In mindfulness meditation, you simply try to become aware of everything that is happening in the universe around you. You try to become absolutely omniscient about what you can see, hear, feel, smell, and taste.

You want to be completely in touch with your senses, and you start by studying your breathing. In this exercise, rather than manipulating your breathing, you simply start by being aware of your breathing. You go, "Oh, that that is what it sounds like when I breathe. That is what it feels like when I breathe."

You begin to notice your heart and your skin and how the floor feels against your feet, or how the chair feels against your legs and bum. You simply become more and more aware of everything your body is experiencing. You are trying to become super sensitive and super aware of the world around you while you just sit there being.

Our bodies are trained to turn off extraneous information. This is why, when you are in a room that smells bad, after a few minutes, you do not notice it anymore; your brain realizes you have absorbed the information, and stops telling you. In this case, we want to tell our brain in this meditation process, "Do not block out anything. For once, I want to hear all the information." It is amazing how much information your body receives at any given time. It would be unbelievably distracting if you were trying to do something else while listening to all this information without prioritizing it.

While you are doing this meditation, this is the perfect time to understand how your body works and to get a little more in touch with how the machine that is your body operates.

When you are practicing your mindfulness meditation, you will notice extraneous thoughts about the past or the future distracting you. If you start thinking about something that happened yesterday or something that might happen later. Just say to those thoughts, "Thank you, but I do not have time for that right now. I appreciate you reminding me, but I will deal with that later. I have something more important I am doing right now." We can acknowledge those thoughts and then push them away, rather than just trying to ignore them and letting those thoughts chase us through our minds.

5. Movement meditation

You may be most familiar with this either as yoga, where you move and meditate at the same time, or tai chi, the Chinese martial art that we often see grandparents practice in the park where they move very slowly. Tai chi is all about extremely precise and slow movements, and while it looks like something only for grandparents, it is super-duper hard. We are used to moving fast, and it takes a lot more precision, focus, and energy to move slowly.

The simplest form of movement meditation is walking meditation. This is where you walk and meditate at the same time as you focus on achieving a bit of relaxation in your mind while you walk. We have already tried this with a few exercises earlier in the book, and it is perfect because you accomplish two things at once.

Taking a walk through the nature, looking at the wonder of the world around you is very meditative. Going for a walk in the park, or even driving a little further and going to a national park where you can see waterfalls and wild animals, is very meditative and peaceful. There is a reason people enjoy getting back to nature; it helps us move away from all the noise and distraction of our lives.

6. Activity-oriented meditation

There are certain activities that you may enjoy, some of which are repetitive and can help you relax your mind, such as painting, knitting, sewing, or drawing. Artistic meditation is great because you relax your mind, you strengthen it, and you also end up with some nice art.

There are many people who take up knitting because it is a slow process: it takes a long time to accomplish something. Each little twitch of the needles only creates one more knot, and it takes thousands or tens of thousands of repetitions to create anything. It is a process that requires both precision and repetition. It is very hard, but many people find it powerful and relaxing.

Some people even find meditation in cooking. What you want is an activity that has pieces that are very repetitive and also takes up all of your mental energy. You have to be focused on what you are doing; you have to be caught in the moment.

I find sports to be very meditative. Most of the sports I practice now are singular sports. Whether I am kayaking, paddling, surfing, or stand-up paddling, in all of these activities it's just me and the universe. I am wrestling the ocean, and as I pull my paddle over and over again in a repetitive motion, my mind is very relaxed; I do not have time to think about anything else.

7. Visualization

This is a very powerful technique that can accelerate your success with the law of attraction. It is where you close your mind, you begin with breathing meditation, and then you focus on the object of your desires.

You start by seeing your mind encompassed by a glowing white light, and piece by piece, you put together a stunningly real visualization in your mind. This can be a mental image of a place, event, person, or anything else.

You want to imagine and create your desires. If you have a specific financial goal, imagine and visualize your life when you have achieved it. Imagine and feel what it looks, smells, sounds, and tastes like when the wealth you are seeking has entered your life.

The more senses you attach to this visualization, the more powerful it becomes. This is how you can send a shining beacon to the universe and bring your entire mind and body into alignment, so that you are now laser-focused on your actual goal.

8. Guided meditation

In this technique, you listen to a speaker take you through a meditation process, so you do not have to do it alone.

These are the meditations that we sometimes hear on the radio or on TV, when they say, "Now imagine yourself walking through a forest; you hear a babbling brook by you, and you see a deer." They tell you what to see and feel, and it helps you as you develop and build this process.

Reflection Questions

1. Have you tried any of these forms of meditation before? Did any of them work for you? Have you learned something new about meditation in this chapter and what do you plan to do the next time you try one of these techniques?

2. Which of these techniques would you define the most intriguing? Why?

3. Which of the meditation techniques above are you excited about trying? Why?

4. Are you nervous about trying any of these techniques? If so, why? How will you overcome this nervousness?

5. What are the most significant things you hope to achieve through meditation?

6. Do you see how meditation will help you to harness more effectively the law of attraction now?

Exercises

1. Brainstorm some images you would like to try to use in your practice of visualization meditation. Try to come up with at least ten good ideas.

2. Choose two of the images you came up with in question 1. For each of these, write how you would bring in the five senses (sight, hearing, taste, touch, and smell).

3. Do a mindfulness meditation every day for at least three days. Early on the fourth day, answer these questions:

   a) Do you feel happier?

   b) Do you feel more in control of your thinking and your mind generally?

c) Do you feel more in control of your life?

4. Think of an activity-oriented meditation that would work for you, and try the activity as meditation at least once. Once you have done this, answer these questions:

a) Are you surprised by how effective this meditation was? Why or why not?

b) Can you think of any other activities that you could use in this way?

10

THE PRINCIPLES OF VISUALIZATION AND MATERIALIZATION

As we discussed earlier, visualization and materialization are extremely important concepts and components of the law of attraction. The things we visualize tend to materialize; this means that the things that we think about the most tend to make an appearance in our life. This is why people who worry about things a lot often have those things happen to them. Our negative thoughts are just as powerful in affecting universes as our positive thoughts.

As with any goal, rather than give you a huge massive task and set you to it, I like to break it into small pieces and teach you piece by piece. You have already learned the process of visualization, and I want to hammer home the lesson by explaining how it all works as part of the law attraction and why we have learned these processes.

It is important to know that even though we call it visualization, we do want to use as many of your senses as possible. For many of us, our sense of smell and taste are more powerful and evoke memories more effectively than our eyes or our ears.

Example: Incorporating the Five Senses

Let's pretend you want to create a visualization of walking along a beautiful beach on a Caribbean Island.

Sight: The sand; the glittering water; the people relaxing; the people wading and swimming in the water.

Sound: Splashing waves; people splashing the water; the cries of seabirds; perhaps people talking in the background.

Touch: The feeling of the water on your hands; sprinkling water landing on you from the ocean waves; the feeling of sand under your feet.

Taste: The taste of sea air; the taste of fresh, revitalizing air.

Smell: The smell of sea air.

Now think of something you want to visualize. This should be something that you hope to manifest in your real life in the future through the power of the law of attraction.

Once you have decided what it is you want to visualize, write down details for each of the categories below. You should complete this exercise in your Law of Attraction Journal.

Sight:
Sound:
Touch:
Taste:
Smell:

Tips for the Most Effective Visualization

1. When creating a visualization, make sure to activate as many of the five senses as possible. When you are visualizing life on a tropical beach, you begin by seeing the sand and the icy blue water, and then you can feel the breeze of

the wind on your skin, the sound of the wind rustling through the palm trees, the sound of the ocean lapping against the shore, and the sun beating on your shoulders. Perhaps you hear a bird making a noise as it flies off in the distance. Then you take a step into the water; you feel the warmth of that tropical ocean, you feel the waves as the water is a little higher and a little lower, and the sand underneath your feet. You can smell that distinctive salty smell of the ocean and a little bit of that pine tree scent in the background. To solidify this, perhaps you grab a piece of pineapple (or even a piña colada), and now you have a tropical drink in your hands; you can feel its coolness against your hand. As you take a bite (or a sip), you can firmly taste the tartness of the pineapple.

2. Always be aware of the powerful connection you have with the universe. Imagination is often the realm where our reality and the reality of the universe mingle. This is where the universe is most likely to receive your signaling and understand your messages. Your voice is louder in your imagination than it is outside your body.

3. Create positive inner dialogues that support your visualizations. If your mind is not in alignment, the messages you send to the universe are not in alignment. You need to achieve total agreement within yourself. This is why we practice meditation to push away those negative thoughts.

Those negative thoughts or bad voices in the back of your mind can distract you in every single stage of this process. When you are visualizing, if you have a little negative voice in there or a negative image, one minute you are relaxing on the beach, and the next minute there is a palm tree falling toward you or something is on fire; you need to silence that voice.

Additionally, we want to go beyond deactivating the negative and activate the positive. Create mental affirmations that are in line with your desire. If you desire is to become a published author and that is the goal you are moving towards, you should say to yourself repeatedly, "I am a published author. I am on the path to author success. I am moving down this path. I am going to succeed. The words I write are words people enjoy."

4. Ensure that your mental images are as bright and vibrant as possible. Use loads of colors and be very expressive. It is better to be too expressive than not expressive enough. In fact, with visualization, you cannot become too expressive. Think about CGI, those computer-generated images we see in movies now. There is a big difference between a cheap movie and expensive movie, and you can tell straight away when they spent almost nothing vs. when they spent a hundred million dollars on computer graphics. The better the graphics are, the more you get pulled into the movie; it becomes more believable. Make sure you use the best special effects possible to go all the way to the top in your mental visualizations.

5. Make sure that you are part of the image. You are not staring at a painting; you are standing inside of the holodeck. Your visualization should be a hologram that

fully surrounds you in every direction, and you are a participant and the star of it. This is far more powerful than imagining that you are standing in front of a wall, looking at a picture. We want to go far beyond that and create a real experience.

6. Boost your mental image with positive emotions. If you put a lot of effort into giving your mental movie the best and most expensive CGI possible, then this part will be quite easy. You should feel peaceful, happy, excited, and energized. Activate as many different emotions as possible in each of your visualizations.

7. Be sure to cultivate and activate your sense of gratitude. If you feel gratitude while you are experiencing this state, you will pull those last negative vestiges and doubts into alignment and turn them into positive beliefs about your desires.

To circle back to our example about the person who wants to achieve wealth and thinks all wealthy people are jerks, if you fully visualize yourself with a wealthy desire, when you add in the attitude of gratitude and see that as a wealthy person you have not changed, your mind comes into alignment.

Finally, your mind goes, "Okay I do not have to block you from achieving wealth anymore because now I know that even if you achieve wealth, you will not become a rich jerk." You are sending a clear signal, and you bring your mind fully into alignment. Just as with our spine in meditation, we want to bring our mind into full alignment. We want to achieve perfect posture both physically and mentally.

8. Practice visualizing daily. The more you practice this, the better you will get, and the more easily you can push away extraneous and distracting thoughts so that your mental image does not shatter with the dumb, irrelevant negative thoughts.

9. Ensure that your emotional state is in alignment. If you visualize yourself on a beach and create a perfect image, but then you attach the emotion of fear to it, you have got a problem. If you imagine yourself on a beach and then you imagine yourself on a beach on the TV show *Lost*, suddenly it does not become that desirable. The last thing you want to do is attach a negative emotion to our experience; make sure you have the correct emotion to go with your visualization.

Ego vs. Authentic Self

Many new students and practitioners of the law of attraction get caught at this point. They cannot separate their egos from their authentic self, so we want to be very clear about what these terms mean and how you can achieve this. In order to achieve maximum success with the law of attraction, your visualizations, your desires, and your goals need to come from your authentic self, not from your ego.

Goals from your ego are often goals that you simply want to achieve for external validation or because other people think that is what you should want. For example, everyone thinks that I should own a house; this what everyone in America does – you buy a house to spend the next twenty years paying it off, and then, when you finally paid it off, your kids move out of the house, and you end up having to sell it and move into a smaller house anyway. Most of us consider buying a house a key step or key moment in adulthood.

Owning a house is not one of my desires because it does not come from my true, authentic self; it is simply the desire of a collective ego. If I bought a house and were tied to a specific location for the next twenty or thirty years, that would be very suffocating for me; even on my paradise island, it is not something I want. I would be pursuing a goal that came from somewhere outside my mind. In order to separate your ego from your authentic self, you want to focus on understanding and being in alignment with your purpose in life. We talked about this early in the book, and now it is coming back. We are circling back to that; we are closing that loop.

We want to cultivate exceptional self-awareness to truly understand who you are and what you desire. How many times did we purchase something simply because we saw it in a commercial, and then when we got it, we realized it was not great? Cars, toys, houses – we think they are going to fulfill us, but we cannot fall into the pattern of seeking external validation.

Instead, focus on things that give your life true meaning. Goals that emanate from your authentic self are ones that support your growth into the person you want to be and fulfill your purpose in life. When I tried to use the law of attraction to draw pure wealth to me, there was always a barrier, because that part is my ego.

When my focus is on writing more books, releasing books faster, and having enough wealth to pay a team to make that happen, then the wealth flows in like a waterfall because the desire for wealth is in alignment with my goals and my authentic self. We can achieve great things that make life better and easier (like wealth, fame, love, and happiness) as long as they are in alignment with your authentic self and your true desires, and are not simply there to impress other people or as an expression of your ego.

Making Time for Visualization

You lead a busy life; so do I. Just this morning, I was working with a new piece of scheduling software. This week, for the first time in over a year, I had ten meetings in one week. In fact, they were over the course of two days only; I have never been so busy. I never have that many meetings; I usually have one a week or even less, as I live in the middle of nowhere.

I am sure you are busy as well, but what I want you to think about is adding a specific time each day for visualization. There are a couple of ways you can do this. You can visualize first thing in the morning when you wake up; that can be your morning activity. Alternatively, you can simply add an alarm to your watch that tells you to visualize at certain times. Design a specific time and a reminder – it is easy to get distracted by life.

As much as we add meetings and other stuff to our schedules and calendars, we can also add things that are important for ourselves. We can add in exercise, alone time, movie time, meditation time, and visualization time. It is okay to use organization to provide relaxation. Once you have made a decision about when you are going to practice visualization, open your Law of Attraction Journal and write down how often you can visualize each week, what time of day you can do it, and how long you want your sessions to last.

At the end of each week, you can check with your notebook and see if you hit your goals or if you have fallen short, and perhaps you need to add a second alert to your watch or phone.

11

RIGHT ACTION

We are getting close to the end of this book. If you read other books on the law of attraction, much of the material in this book may be familiar to you. This chapter is the one that is often missing from other books, and it is the reason why I felt the need to write this book and share it with you.

Many people treat the law of attraction like a magic spell, but by now, hopefully, you can see the mechanics of the process. While we use language such as "sending a message to the universe," hopefully you can see now that I do not just mean a metaphysical message between me and the moon, but what I mean is bringing all of your thoughts and your conscious and subconscious mind into alignment.

Every day, we make thousands of tiny decisions, and those decisions are built upon our beliefs. When you believe that you will fail in a project and someone offers you a new job, you will turn it down; a little belief that you are not good enough can dramatically affect you.

The law of attraction does not just bring you wealth and success through magic and extraordinary efforts. Instead, what will happen as your body and mind are in alignment is that you will act like a person who can achieve the things you want to achieve.

Often, it is not the world holding you back but your own thoughts. When you believe that you could be an author and you start to act like one, your belief becomes stronger. You will write that book, and when you talk to publishers, you will talk like a real author, and they go, "Yeah let us do this. We are going to publish you."

I just had a meeting with a large publisher last week, and a big part of the conversation was all about my confidence as a writer. If I showed any lack of confidence or acted like someone who was not a writer, the conversation would have gone down the wrong path. Because I believed in myself, I have written many best-selling books. Before I finished my first book, I needed that belief in place. If I had believed my first book would fail, I would have never written it.

That is not to say that I was without fear and nervousness. Of course, I was nervous that people would not like it, but I still pushed it out there because I believed it was the best that I could do. Strong beliefs and the right actions can overcome these little fears. Before we even worry about affecting the universe with our thoughts, we need to make sure that we affect our behaviors. If you say to your mind and to the universe, "I want wealth," but when your boss offers you overtime you turn it down, your actions and your thoughts are not in alignment, and the universe will ignore you.

The universe believes in cooperative behavior. The person who works harder gets rewarded, and the person who demonstrates their willingness to make things happen gets the final prize. Fortune truly does favor the bold. Stop hoping for a magical result.

Sometimes, the universe will simply bring you a job offer, and if you turn it down because you want the universe to instead bring you a giant chest of pirate treasure, then you are going to be left wanting. The universe is not a big fan of knocking multiple times.

The world around us operates based on the path of least resistance. If the easiest way to increase your income is to get you a new job, that is going to happen far easier than the universe trying to manifest a pirate treasure and bring it directly to your house. It is very hard to move a treasure chest across countries to your front door without anyone noticing it. It is far easier for a friend to say, "If you are looking for a job, we have an opening, and we will pay you twenty percent more than what you make right now."

Which one is more realistic? The job offer. Which one is more exciting and you wish you could tell everyone about? The pirate treasure chest. This is where people falter with the law of attraction. Opportunities come their way, and they reject them. "No thanks, I am going to wait for the universe to provide." But the universe says, "Who do you think brought you a job offer?" Be careful about the opportunities that you reject and turn down. If you want to lose weight but refuse to go to the gym, guess what? You are not going to lose weight.

Share Your Success

The law of attraction only works when it is combined with the right action. Your subconscious, conscious, mind, and body need to be in alignment.

You need to believe that being skinnier is better than

being fat; you need to have the desire to lose that weight, and you need to take action. The universe will only accelerate the process. I know you are thinking, "Jonathan, what are you doing to me? That sounds hard. The law of attraction is supposed to be easy!" And that is why people buy those other the law of attraction books and never achieve anything. I do not want to give you something that is easy to sell but does not work; I would rather be honest with you.

More than anything else, bad beliefs hold people back from success in life. Bad information and bad beliefs are often the cause of our misfortunes. Fixing your beliefs, your understanding of the universe and your desires, correcting false beliefs, and replacing bad information with good information are the first steps in understanding what you want from the universe; only then can you start to make those things happen.

For example, if your desire is to live on a tropical island, my first question to you is always going to be: how much does that life cost? If you do not know the answer, I know you are not in alignment with yourself. Someone who truly wants to live on a tropical island will have pictures of a tropical island on a wall in their room, they will have a visualization board, they will know which island they want to go to, how much the plane tickets cost, and the cost of living there. This is what I did five and ten years ago, and here I am.

Even in my early twenties, I was looking online to see how much it cost to buy your own island. I was looking at how much it cost to buy and run your own hotel on different islands. I looked at the cost of living, the visa process, the complexity of moving money around, and the safety and dangers of different countries. I know the cost of living on most islands in the world.

Yes, I live on a tropical island now, but guess what? I have about seven backups ranked in order of first to last choice, and I have certain conditions that can trigger me if I realize I need to move back to the United States. I know exactly where I am going to move to, and I know what the cost of living is there. I look at rental and house prices in Hawaii at least once a year. I look at Internet speeds in different countries. All of these little research steps are a demonstration that I am in alignment. That is how you go from a metaphysical, mystical goal to an actionable, achievable goal. This is the right action.

When you begin to implement this book, before you leave any reviews or tell your friends whether this book was amazing or garbage, please complete all the activities. Take time to implement the right actions. If you message me in the Facebook group or email me, I will be happy to talk to you, but the first thing I will ask you is if you have actually done this. If you have not combined the right action with your belief, then I do not expect the universe to give it to you. You have broken the rules.

If you have something in your life you want, make sure you do enough research first. The little things we do not think about because we do not research can become big problems. Of course, if you are a millionaire, you can afford to buy boats all over town, and when one breaks, you just buy a new one, but that is not the mindset we want to cultivate.

As you move forward and think about where this process is going to take you, remember that this is a cooperative venture. The law of attraction is an active principle; it is not passive. You do not push a button and wait for your results. You have to cooperate with the universe, and then take the right action. Now that we are the end of this book, it is time to take the right actions. The first right action is to build and fill out a Law of Attraction Journal.

The second right action is to participate and complete all of the activities in this book; every exercise and every activity is there for a reason. If you read this book quickly, then go back and work your way through the book, and do the activities.

The third right action is for you to leave an honest and detailed review. Your feedback means a lot to me. If you felt something was missing from the book, you can email me or message me on Facebook and let me know. I will work to improve the book and clarify or add extra activities and exercises. My goal is to trigger change more than it is to sell books. Please stay in alignment with me as much as you try to stay in line with the universe and let us work together.

You now have the tools and the understanding to achieve more with your life and make more amazing things happen. I am very excited about that. We have covered a lot of material in this book, and you may need to read it two or three times to absorb each different technique and piece of information. If you have any questions, or if you feel stuck anywhere, please join our special Facebook tribe. It is free, it is where I communicate with my audience, and you can find other people on the same path as you to share guidance, wisdom, and experiences. Together, we can encourage you and help you find success.

You are a member of my tribe now because you purchased this book. Even if you grabbed it on Kindle Unlimited or you downloaded it from a naughty website, that is okay. We are in a cooperative venture together, and if you are willing to put in the effort, I am willing to work with you. Reach out if you have any questions and please leave that review for me. I am an independent author who supports my family with the words that I write. If you are on a Kindle device, just go to the next page and click that little fifth star.

That allows me to help more people and increases my effect on the universe. It also puts a little "plus one" in your karma column! You earn a little point from the universe, and that is going to come back to you full circle.

You never know what might come your way when you put positive energy into the universe. As amazing things happen for you and the law of attraction begins to manifest those very things you visualized, I would like you to take pictures of them.

Take a picture of you with your new car or in front of your new house with your family and share those pictures on Amazon or in the Facebook group or email me so that I can get a little bit encouragement and feel excited about your success. As much as you invested in me by reading this book, I am now invested in you, and I cannot wait to see the success that is coming your way.

LET'S SOAR TOGETHER

The hardest part of personal growth is going it alone. When you are in isolation, the night can seem too dark, and success can seem so far away.

We often quit right before we could experience our biggest success. Join something bigger than yourself where you can get the support, feedback, and guidance you need to achieve your desired success.

Please join my FREE, private Facebook group, filled with supportive people on the same path.

https://servenomaster.com/community

This is a great place to chat with me daily, share your experiences with the exercises and find a supportive group of people who are all on the same journey as you.

MORE INFORMATION

Throughout this book, I mentioned other books, images, links, and additional content. All of that can be found at:

https://servenomaster.com/lawofattraction

You don't have to worry about trying to remember any other links or the names of anything mentioned in this book. Just enjoy the journey and focus on taking control of your destiny.

FOUND A TYPO?

While every effort goes into ensuring that this book is flawless, it is inevitable that a mistake or two will slip through the cracks.

If you find an error of any kind in this book, please let me know by visiting:

ServeNoMaster.com/typos

I appreciate you taking the time to notify me. This ensures that future readers never have to experience that awful typo. You are making the world a better place.

ABOUT THE AUTHOR

Born in Los Angeles, raised in Nashville, educated in London, Jonathan Green has spent years wandering the globe as his own boss – but it didn't come without a price. Like most people, he struggled through years of working in a vast, unfeeling bureaucracy.

After the backstabbing and gossip of the university system threw him out of his job, he was devastated – stranded far away from home without a paycheck coming in. Despite having to hang on to survival with his fingernails, he didn't just survive; he thrived.

Today, he says that getting fired with no safety net was the best thing that ever happened to him. Despite the stress, it gave him an opportunity to rebuild and redesign his life.

One year after being on the edge of financial ruin, Jonathan had replaced his job, working as a six-figure SEO consultant. With his Rolodex overflowing with local businesses and their demands getting higher and higher, he knew that he had to take his hands off the wheel.

That's one of the big takeaways from his experience. Lifestyle design can't just be about a job replacing income, because often, you're replicating the stress and misery that comes with that lifestyle too!

Thanks to smart planning and personal discipline, he started from scratch again, with a focus on repeatable, passive income that created lifestyle freedom. He was more successful than he could have possibly expected. He traveled the world, helped friends and family, and moved to an island in the South Pacific.

Now, he's devoted himself to breaking down every hurdle entrepreneurs face at every stage of their progress, from developing mental strength and resilience in the depths of depression and anxiety, to developing financial and business literacy, to building a concrete plan to escape the 9-to-5, all the way down to the nitty-gritty details of teaching what you need to build a business of your own.

In a digital world packed with "experts," there are few people with the experience to tell you how things really work, why they work and what actually works in the online business world.

Jonathan doesn't just have the experience; he has it in a variety of spaces. A bestselling author, a "ghostwriter to the gurus" who commands sky-high rates due to his ability to deliver captivating work in a hurry, and a video producer who helps small businesses share their skills with their communities.

He's also the founder of the Serve No Master podcast, a weekly show focused on financial independence, networking with the world's most influential people, writing epic stuff online and traveling the world for cheap.

Altogether, it makes him one of the most captivating and accomplished people in the lifestyle design world, sharing the best of what he knows with total transparency, as part of a mission to free regular people from the 9-to-5 and live on their own terms.

Learn from his successes and failures and Serve No Master.

Find out more about Jonathan at:
ServeNoMaster.com

BOOKS BY JONATHAN GREEN

Non-Fiction

Serve No Master Series

Serve No Master

Serve No Master (French)

Breaking Orbit

20K a Day

Control Your Fate

BREAKTHROUGH (coming soon)

Habit of Success Series

PROCRASTINATION

Influence and Persuasion

Overcome Depression

Stop Worrying and Anxiety

Love Yourself

Conquer Stress

Law of Attraction

Mindfulness and Meditation Ultimate Guide

Meditation Techniques for Beginners

Social Anxiety and Shyness Ultimate Guide

Coloring Depression Away with Adult Coloring Books

Don't be Quiet

Develop Good Habits with S.J. Scott

How to Quit Your Smoking Habit

The Weight Loss Habit

Seven Secrets

Seven Networking Secrets for Jobseekers

Biographies

The Fate of my Father

Complex Adult Coloring Books

The Dinosaur Adult Coloring Book

The Dog Adult Coloring Book

The Celtic Adult Coloring Book

The Outer Space Adult Coloring Book

Irreverent Coloring Books

Dragons Are Bastards

Fiction

Gunpowder and Magic

The Outlier (As Drake Blackstone)

ONE LAST THING

Reviews are the lifeblood of any book on Amazon, especially for the independent author. If you would click five stars on your Kindle device or visit this special link at your convenience, that will ensure that I can continue to produce more books. A quick rating or review helps me to support my family, and I deeply appreciate it.

Without stars and reviews, you would never have found this book. Please take just thirty seconds of your time to support an independent author by leaving a rating.

Thank you so much!

To leave a review go to ->

https://servenomaster.com/lawreview

Sincerely,
Jonathan Green
ServeNoMaster.com

www.ingramcontent.com/pod-product-compliance
Lightning Source LLC
Chambersburg PA
CBHW060045230426
43661CB00004B/669